# DID DAVID HASSELHOFF END THE COLD WAR?

# 50 FACTS YOU NEED TO KNOW: Europe

# DID DAVID HASSELHOFF END THE COLD WAR?

## 50 FACTS YOU NEED TO KNOW: Europe

### Emma Hartley

ICON BOOKS

This edition published in the UK in 2007
by Icon Books Ltd, The Old Dairy,
Brook Road, Thriplow,
Cambridge SG8 7RG
email: info@iconbooks.co.uk
www.iconbooks.co.uk

Originally published in 2006 as
50 Facts You Need to Know: Europe

Reprinted 2006

Sold in the UK, Europe, South Africa and Asia
by Faber & Faber Ltd, 3 Queen Square,
London WC1N 3AU
or their agents

Distributed in the UK, Europe, South Africa and Asia
by TBS Ltd, TBS Distribution Centre, Colchester Road
Frating Green, Colchester CO7 7DW

Published in Australia in 2007
by Allen & Unwin Pty Ltd,
PO Box 8500, 83 Alexander Street,
Crows Nest, NSW 2065

Distributed in Canada by
Penguin Books Canada,
90 Eglinton Avenue East, Suite 700,
Toronto, Ontario M4P 2YE

ISBN 10: 1-84046-794-0
ISBN 13: 978-1-840467-94-9

Extract from *Colossus* by Niall Ferguson (Penguin Books, 2004, 2005)
reproduced by permission of Penguin Books Ltd.

Extract from *Why Switzerland?* by Jonathan Steinberg (2nd edition)
reproduced by permission of Cambridge University Press.

Extract from *The Accursed Mountains* reprinted by permission of
HarperCollins Publishers Ltd © (Robert Carver) (1999).

Typesetting by Hands Fotoset

Printed and bound in the UK by
Bookmarque Ltd, Croydon, Surrey

# Contents

# Acknowledgements

I would like to thank Zia Sardar, who apparently specialises in finding young authors for Icon books, for giving me a metaphorical kick up the bum and making this possible. And several of my colleagues at *The Times* for their thoughtful help and guidance: Anjana Gadgil, Robin Ash, Raj Hegde and, more than anyone, Vince Ryan. See you down The Caxton. Thank you David Cohen for moral support and lunch, Regina for translation and her many other works, Hugh Barnes for crucial information about Stockard Channing, Sheridan and Max for taking me ice-skating, and Mum and Dad for the chapter about the disappearing island in the Azores … because you have to start somewhere.

Other thanks go to Richard Whitman at Chatham House, Dr Mary Hilsom, Adrian Strittmatter because you should never ignore a man whose own government forces him to possess an automatic weapon, Stephen Brown from AFP in Copenhagen, all at the Warburg Institute, Dominique at the University College London press office, Nora Harding and Sue Gurney for giving me such a warm welcome, Tim Pharaoh of the British Geological Survey, Professor Willem Gellar, Martin Jay at *The Sprout*, Brian Thynne at the National Maritime Museum, Rowan Pelling and Dr Tuppy Owens for being women after my own heart, Jack Gottschalk, Lucy Leonhardt and Andrew Furlow at Icon, and everyone else who helped out.

# About the author

Emma Hartley is a journalist and author. She has worked for the *Daily Telegraph*, the *Evening Standard*, the *Independent* (as a leader writer and as a reporter) and *The Times*.

# Introduction

Every conceivable definition of Europe has been used in the writing of this book: geographic, political, psychological, you name it – it's in here. Similarly, the approach to what constitutes a fact has been a bit on the laissez-faire side. For this I make very few apologies – although I owe sympathy, at least, to any Albanians who take issue with my method (see Chapter 7).

Despite having studied 'Europe' at university and then soaking up what was available in print, on television and the radio, when it came to having an opinion on the European Union at the outset of researching *50 Facts,* I was confused in a pretty unique way. The subject remained elusive. I couldn't help feeling that somehow I didn't have the *right* information.

At college, 'Europe' had been a bafflingly dull course, all about bureaucracy and treaties. There were no big ideas with which to grapple: no ideological compass except something called 'the European Dream', which was presented as something unavoidably Belgian and therefore, as I say, baffling.

Later, at the *Daily Telegraph* it was normal to sneer at all things European, at the *Independent* to admire them. But at neither was it clear how they had arrived at these positions or how everyone else knew what to think: it just seemed too large a subject. (Looking back on it, this troubles me slightly since I was a leader writer for a while at the *Independent*.) So my previous experience of the subject was probably quite typical: I wanted to understand, but didn't really feel I had the tools. Researching and writing this book has given me an opportunity to assemble some: flint arrowheads or nanotechnology? You decide.

Most of my biggest problems previously came, I think, from unconsciously dealing with the European Union as something abstracted from reality. It's a political idea but it's also a place where people live. While this sounds obvious, it helped me, as a grumpy Anglo-Saxon, to think of it as a physical reality and also explains why many of these 'facts' do not appear remotely political at first glance.

I've never been a great believer in deciding that some things are political and others are not, though. It's not that I can't make a distinction for practicality's sake, it's just that suspicion descends about the motives of those who divide the world into 'this part that concerns me' and 'that part does not', which is most frequently the purpose that such labels serve. In this sense, David Hasselhoff in all his glory, is the emblem for the book as well as its hearth god. All hail The Hoff! May your chest hair gleam in perpetuity.

So what have I learned? Well, despite having had doubts about which way I would fall in the so-called European debate, I have to admit that familiarity did not breed contempt. I've come across European institutions that need a lot of work and EU officials who should certainly be fired (as well as a couple who shouldn't have been, see Chapter 47) – but I've also grown respect for some of the wider mechanisms involved. In particular, EU expansion seems to be a civilising project in the Enlightenment mould: bringing clean, running water, among other things, to places where previously there was none (see Chapter 33 on Romania). This must surely be a good thing?

I've also realised that the dull, buzzing sensation in the head that most people get when the subject of the EU comes up performs an actual *function*: their attention glides away – and this has been the case for a great many years – because it suits everyone. The European Union was created in an undemocratic way, top-down, of which good, democracy-loving Europeans should probably disapprove. The moral ambiguities that this involves – especially after a century during which Europe suffered terribly as a result of totalitarianism – do explain why the subject is often seen as too complex to bother with. It also explains why, for so many years, the braying Europhobe voices in Britain's unrepresentatively right-wing press drowned out my understanding of the issues by focusing relentlessly on the negative.

But these Europhobe voices had, and have, many good and valid points to make. It's simply that very few of the points have anything to do with federalism, straight bananas or metric martyrs – the hoary old standards of the British media's European reper-toire. Good things can come of dubious beginnings. The reality – call it a fact if you would like – is that the EU exists and we live in it.

If you would like to take issue with any of the above, please direct all comments and remarks to Christopher Booker c/o the *Sunday Telegraph*.

# There is a railway in Hungary run by children

A train set is a delight for many adults, so try to imagine how much fun the Children's Railway in the Buda Hills outside Budapest gives its under-age workers.

It was dreamt up in 1946 as a project for the newly Communist country's Young Pioneer movement, constructed to link a large Pioneers' camp in the Buda Hills with other public transport. More than 9,000 children aged ten to fourteen have been involved since it opened in 1950, taking tickets, cashing up, waving flags and even driving its full-sized trains on the seven mile narrow-gauge track.

'I went to work there when I was ten', said Zsuzsanna Kiss, 35. Now a sales manager at a computer company in Budapest, she looks back on her days at the Children's Railway with nostalgia.

'I had been a hard worker at elementary school and I had a friend on my street who was already involved. We used to swap the jobs around so everyone got to do everything eventually. There were fifteen groups of us, so we had a day there every fifteen days.'

'We had a special suit and tie, and working there was supposed to promote our accuracy and discipline. But although it was a specifically Communist project it was wonderful fun too. You should see how beautiful those hills are', she sighed.

The 'elite' children of Budapest went through a tough selection to get there. First their academic performance was taken into account, and then they received the same training as adult railway workers. Because there were no adults at the intermediate stations along the track, they were in charge of the train – a large amount of responsibility at a young age.

The Children's Railway became popular, attracting domestic tourism and school trips from all over the country. Everyone went to marvel at the seven stations, two depots, the horseshoe-shaped tunnel and young workers, as well as the natural beauty of the area.

The Pioneer movement withdrew from the railway's day-to-day running after ten years, but the railway continued to provide excellent propaganda for the Hungarian regime. Then, as now, one picture of a smiling child is worth a thousand words. When the Cold War ended, the railway had a few up-and-down years, but it's now back on track, so to speak, as a tourist attraction, although it is very expensive to maintain.

The extraordinary idea of a railway run by children became a reality because of Communism. Who else but a Communist government would build a railway – a mode of transport notorious the world over for being prone to financial catastrophe – for the sole purpose of propaganda?

The Young Pioneers began in Russia after the 1917 revolution, as a replacement for the Scout movement, which was outlawed for being 'bourgeois' and its proponents arrested and interned. Wherever another country became Communist, the Pioneer movement went too. It still exists today in China, North Korea, Vietnam and Cuba.

Among other things, it allowed regimes hungry for personal information about their people to insert themselves into youngsters' lives. Authorities kept a watchful eye over Young Pioneers and selected suitable candidates when they turned fourteen for the Young Communists' League. Having been a Young Communist was of enormous help getting a good job as an adult.

It was argued by the Soviets that the Scout movement in the West does something similar: turns out useful young men and women, who believe in doing their bit for society and participating in the mainstream of their country's life. After all, children are impressionable, so any conscientious social engineer should catch them while they're young.

Zsuzsanna Kiss's nostalgia for her childhood complicates her relationship with the old Communist regime. Her first experience of it, at the Children's Railway, was exhilarating, character-forming and a matter of some personal pride that she had been accepted. As an adult she knows why the regime ended, but her happy Communist childhood remains a part of her, a relic that will die when she does, and knowing this must give her memories an additional poignancy.

A longing for the Communist past in Eastern Europe has become something of a phenomenon, especially since the film *Goodbye Lenin!* did so well all over the world. It was the story of a mother who fell into a coma shortly before the end of the Cold War. When she awoke several months later, her children were warned that any shocks could kill her, so they set about reconstructing the world around her bedroom in the style of the former East Germany.

In the film, *Ostalgia* – coined after the German word *Ost* for East – seemed to revolve around the children presenting various consumer items to their bedridden mother, memorably a particular kind of cucumber pickle, while simultaneously trying to shield her from the massive Coca-Cola advertisement being erected outside her bedroom window.

This kitsch approach to politics was ironic in the sense that the film conveyed the opposite message to what it literally appeared to be. The focus on consumerism demonstrated that this was at the heart of the film-makers' concerns, even as they simultaneously suggested that the Communist past (no consumerism) was not as bad as it seemed at the time. The film's subtle charm also dovetailed with a fashion when it was released for all things retro and specifically 1980s in the West. It made *Ostalgia* seem a natural, if rather superficial, result of the end of the former German Democratic Republic (GDR).

Some young Germans had adopted the fashion of wearing the GDR's hammer and sickle as a motif and a series of East German-themed television programmes, including one simply called *The GDR Show*, were being aired at the time of the film's release, although there was a clamour of controversy surrounding them. As one member of parliament, Gunter Nooke, asked provocatively: 'Why not have a *Third Reich Show*?'

East Germany is a special case in the former Eastern bloc – it is the only country that subsequently and very abruptly ceased to exist, disappearing without its former citizens having had a proper chance to mourn its passing. Whereas the former Yugoslavia disintegrated into its original constituent parts, East Germany was absorbed by West Germany, which immediately began sending Deutschmarks east. This had the effect of making East Germans, the *Ostländers*, feel like second-class citizens. They didn't have many of the skills needed to make it in their new economy, but were given few of the incentives that, say, the Estonians had, to help them adjust to their new conditions of life ('sink or swim'). In the absence of a clear new beginning, *Ostalgia* became a kind of unfocused melancholy for the past ... and people have said 'things are not what they used to be' ever since they had a language in which to say it.

So in an attempt to place the warm glow of *Ostalgia* in context, consider Pavlik Morozov, who will be forever fourteen years old – he is immortalised in statuary all over the former Soviet bloc. He was adopted as the patron 'saint' of the Young Pioneer movement after being murdered in 1932, apparently for denouncing his father to Stalin's secret police. There are several different accounts of why he denounced his father, out there on a collective farm at Gerasimovka in Siberia. But he was most likely killed by a disgusted member of his own family and was subsequently lionised by Stalin, who said that he embodied all of the qualities that a good Communist child should have. Not to put too fine a point on it, Morozov was a sneak who had his own father interned and this was the example that all Young Pioneers were intended to emulate.

It wasn't that much like the Scouts.

# The European Union is a unique empire

Jacques Delors once famously described the EU as an 'unidentified political object', which made him sound much pithier than usual but also as if he had mistaken it for something mysterious and fascinating – the political equivalent, perhaps, of Catherine Deneuve.

It may have something of the femme fatale about it for those also fascinated by train timetables, but his aphorism points to a big theme of political life, in Britain at least.

As a nation, we have quite a strong aversion to abstractions. If you asked somebody a question about themselves in a pub and they turned to you and said, with no hint of irony, 'I am what I am', collectively we might be inclined to want to slap them ... or at least to spill their drink in such a way that it would cause them mild inconvenience.

Yet this is nearly exactly what the European Union has been implying by omission for a great many years. It's not that we don't know what it's for precisely, or that we're unfamiliar with the major pros and cons ... well, not totally unfamiliar. Or even that we're uninterested. Not entirely so, anyway.

It's just that, for some reason, we don't seem to have the right information to feel comfortable about it: it hasn't adequately explained itself. How could we, the practical British, with centuries of experience in empire building, empire losing, roast meat consumption and beer drinking, get our thoughts around something so conceptually slippery? What's in it for us? The simple absence of a major European war for 60 years feels somehow unsatisfying and insufficiently concrete because, at heart, we are a nation of happy warriors.

So where are the British equivalents to Jacques Delors's pronouncement? A hardy Anglo-Saxon description of what it is that we've got ourselves into? You can guarantee that had there been any, they would have had less of the Catherine Deneuves about them and probably more of the Hugh Grants and the Winston Churchills (since I seem to be dealing in national stereotypes ...).

Perhaps something along the lines of: 'Um, excuse me. Would you mind terribly if we didn't have to fight them on the beaches any more?'

The EU is pretty mysterious to most of us: it was designed that way, top-down. How could it have been otherwise? There have been years of wrangling behind closed doors in Brussels, but to start to make sense of it, we need to know the broad outcome of those meetings and then focus on why we should be interested. That way at least we may end up with something we can use; a way of thinking about Europe that makes sense.

So how would this be for a proposition? The EU is an empire. Not an empire like the Roman, the British or Byzantine Empires necessarily: they were different from each other and the EU is different again. But it's an empire nonetheless, and one that's being built even as we read about it in newspapers and wonder what on earth is going on.

Wonderfully, it's also an empire which has a unique defining characteristic – it has client countries, or 'colonies' in the economic sense, lining up to join, doing the diplomatic equivalent of shouting: 'Me too! Take me next!' It's an empire that other people think is working well – well enough to want to join.

It's true that imperialism has acquired a bad name for itself in certain quarters: you don't have to be a Marxist in order to use the term as a denunciation, although it helps.

But because the European Union isn't an empire in the traditional sense, its brand of imperialism is also different. There are no jackboots, no gulag, no glory of Rome (although it remains a very stylish city). There is very little jingoism associated with this empire at all.

And perhaps because of this, we could take a little pride in wresting the terminology back again. Just because the Russians and Chinese used 'imperialist' as a term of abuse against the West during the Cold War, we don't have to let them get away with it. After all, many would say that the Soviet Union and the People's Republic of China were empires in their own right – indeed, in China's case, that it still is.

Niall Ferguson, in his book *Colossus: the Rise and Fall of America's Empire*, makes a good case for the United States being an empire, even though its national DNA – its history as a former colony – makes it unlikely to accept this description of itself without a fight. However, since it's evidently not averse to a fight (Afghanistan and Iraq have proved this recently), why not press the point?

What else would you call a military superpower with unprecedented wealth and cultural influence, which doesn't hesitate to draw new countries into its orbit? As Ferguson says: 'The Second World War merely saw the defeat of three would-be empires – German, Japanese and Italian – by an alliance between the old West European empires (principally the British, since the others were so swiftly beaten) and two newer empires – that of the Soviet Union and that of the United States.'

*The Times Atlas of World History* describes, among other things, a sequence of 70 empires that have existed throughout human history, beginning with the Akkadian Empire of Mesopotamia circa 2350–2150 BC. Ferguson argues that this list should finish with the United States at number 68, China at 69 and possibly the EU at 70. Also in there are the Haitian Empire, which existed from 1804 to 1806, and the Korean Empire, from 1897 to 1910. There are plenty more that most of us have never heard of.

So why not call the EU an empire? The most obvious problem is that militarily it's not very impressive. In recent years, problems in Bosnia and Kosovo for instance, at the heart of Europe, have been effectively delegated to the US to sort out.

But the whole point of the Pan-Europe movement (as it was originally called in 1923 by Count Richard Coudenhove-Kalergi in his utopian book by that name) is that it should prevent European nations being a danger to each other militarily, so perhaps a certain EU reticence about war isn't surprising. Anyway, how impressive could the Haitian Empire's army have been, and who says that all empires have to be the same?

European Union imperial power is 'soft' power. The EU exemplifies how to get what you want without force, using the abilities to persuade, entice and attract. It arises in large part from its cultural and social values, and the economic life that those values make possible. It has hundreds of thousands of new immigrants every year whose presence attests to the EU's attractive power in these respects. And soft power comes cheaper than military might. Why storm around the world imposing your own values when you can wait for the world to come to you?

My point is this: an empire can be liberal. Why not? An empire can be welcoming and modern. An empire can be attractive. And above all, choosing to see an empire for what it is can be illuminating when it comes to understanding what you are looking at.

# The French defence establishment believes that the existence of UFOs is 'quasi-certain'

On 30 March 1990, two Belgian F16s were scrambled after repeated attempts failed to identify an aircraft flying over the south of the country. When the pilots first locked on to the object it was at 7,000 feet, but within seconds it climbed to 10,000 feet then, incredibly, plummeted to 500 feet in only five seconds.

At the same time the craft accelerated to more than 1,000 miles an hour, or one-and-a-half times the speed of sound. All of this was recorded using instruments on board the F16s and military tracking equipment on the ground. As the object broke the sound barrier there was no sonic boom, and that combination of acceleration and descent would have been fatal to a human pilot.

An American documentary in a series called *Unsolved Mysteries*, made for the Discovery Channel in 1991, interviewed Major General W.J.L. de Brouwer, the chief of operations of the Belgian airforce at the time of the incident. He confirmed: 'We measured some exceptional accelerations which cannot be related to conventional aircraft … The data on all this, which was registered during the lockons on the radar, was totally outside the normal performance envelope of any aeroplane.'

In June 2005, Colonel Daniel de Cock, the military attaché at the Belgian Embassy in London, told me that he knew the General, that he was familiar with the interview he had given, and that there was no suggestion that the General was out of step with the rest of the military establishment.

Back in 1981, on 13 January, Lieutenant Colonel Charles Halt, the deputy base commander of RAF Bentwaters/Woodbridge in Suffolk (an American base), wrote a memo for the British Ministry of Defence (MOD) about a series of incidents at night-time between Christmas and New Year 1980–81. A copy of the memo was released through the US Freedom of Information Act (FOIA) in 1983.

It reported that early in the morning of 27 December 1980, two US airforce security patrolmen went to investigate some unusual lights outside the back gate of RAF Woodbridge in Rendlesham forest. 'The individuals reported seeing a strange glowing object in the forest. The object was described as being metallic in appearance and triangular in shape, approximately two to three metres across the base and approximately two metres high. It illuminated the entire forest with a white light', the memo reads.

'The object itself had a pulsing red light on top and a bank(s) of blue lights underneath. The object was hovering on legs. As the patrolmen approached the object, it manoeuvred through the trees and disappeared ... The next day three depressions one-and-a-half inches deep and seven inches in diameter were found where the object had been sited on the ground. The following night the area was checked for radiation. Beta/gamma readings of 0.1 milliroentgens were recorded with peak readings in the three depressions and near the centre of the triangle formed by the depressions.' This was ten times the expected level of radiation.

The memo goes on to describe how later, on the night of 29 December, a red 'sun-like' light was seen through the trees, throwing off glowing particles before breaking into five separate white pieces and disappearing. For two or three hours after that, three objects were visible in the sky, one of which, to the south, beamed down a stream of light from time to time. 'Numerous individuals, including the undersigned' (himself) 'witnessed the activities', concluded Lieutenant Colonel Halt.

An MOD official called Nick Pope directed me to this document, which is available on the MOD website at www.mod.uk/linked_files/publications/foi/ufo/ufofilepart1.pdf.

Mr Pope once had the job of manning the MOD's UFO desk and has written several books on the subject, as well as the foreword for a book about Rendlesham called *You Can't Tell the People*, by journalist Georgina Bruni. This book claims that the unexplained lights at Rendlesham are the world's 'only officially recognised UFO sighting'.

'Ironically, the claim about Rendlesham being the world's only officially recognised UFO sighting falls down', said Mr Pope, 'not because of any lack of official engagement, but because there are plenty of *other* UFO sightings where the reports are made by military witnesses, or where corroboration of visual sightings is obtained on radar. That said, none of this implies officialdom accepts an extraterrestrial explanation for any UFO sightings.' Not in Britain, anyway.

On 16 July 1999, the French government's Institut des hautes études de défense nationale (IHEDN) – or Institute of Higher Studies for National Defence – published a report called 'UFOs and Defence. What must we be prepared for?'. The report has a preface by General Bernard Norlain of the French airforce, the former director of the IHEDN. The preamble is by André Lebeau, the former president of the Centre national d'études spatiales (CNES) – or the National Centre for Space Studies, which is the French equivalent of NASA. General Denis Letty, also of the French airforce, presided over the auditors on the committee – a *Who's Who* of the French military establishment, although many are retired. The group was called COMETA, which stands for committee for in-depth studies, and their 90-page report took three years to produce.

Its main theme is that 'the accumulation of well-documented observations compels us now to consider all hypotheses as to the origin of UFOs, especially extra-terrestrial hypotheses'.

It presents fifteen individual cases, including nine documented by the French military and one at RAF Lakenheath. An English summary of the report says: 'Although the selection is limited, it seems to be sufficient to convince an informed but open-minded reader of the reality of UFOs.' The French Embassy in London directed me to this report, which is available at www.netowne. com/ufos/important/cometa.htm.

The report also introduces two counter-examples of UFO hoaxes and explains that hoaxes are rare and easily detected. Some non-scientific theories about UFOs are put aside, such as conspiracy and manipulation by very secret, powerful groups, para-psychic phenomena, and collective hallucinations. The hypothesis of secret weapons, it says, is also regarded as very improbable, leaving us with 'various extraterrestrial hypotheses'.

It moves on to discuss the position of the United States on the subject, noting that 'it is still one of denial, more precisely that there is no threat to national security. Actually, declassified documents, released under the FOIA, show another story, one of surveillance of nuclear installations by UFOs, and the continued study of UFOs by the military and intelligence agencies.'

COMETA's report discusses the possible motivations of extra-terrestrial visitors, particularly since they apparently take a keen interest in sites associated with nuclear missiles. It points out that the attitude of the US to all this has been 'most strange', since the incident at Roswell in 1947, which the US initially handled with comparative openness.

'Since that time a policy of increasing secrecy seems to have been applied, which might be explained by the protection at all costs of military technological superiority to be acquired from the study of UFOs', the report says. It suggests that European states and the European Union should try quiet diplomacy towards the US over the issue.

The key question of the report is then arrived at: what should governments prepare for when it comes to UFOs? It runs through the possibilities – that extraterrestrials want to make contact, invade or attack us – although it believes the last two are impro-bable. It also approaches the political and religious ramifications of accepting that the Earth is being visited by an alien culture, and asks how, if the roles were reversed, human beings would handle making contact with a less advanced civilisation elsewhere?

It concludes that 'the physical reality of UFOs, under control of intelligent beings is "quasi-certain". Only one hypothesis takes into account the available data: the hypothesis of extra-terrestrial visitors.'

I began looking into this subject thinking that there may be some places in Europe more prone to UFO sightings than others and that this would mean that these places were loopier than others. This government-produced material is what I found instead. It's hard not to be disturbed by the implications.

DID DAVID HASSELHOFF END THE COLD WAR?

# David Hasselhoff had a role in ending the Cold War

David Hasselhoff had a hit song called 'Looking for Freedom', which was a cover of a German hit from the 1970s called 'Auf Der Strasse Nach Suden'. Already a pop star in Austria and Switzerland, 'The Hoff' was suddenly also huge in Germany.

With its lamenting refrain – 'I've been lookin' for freedom/I've been lookin' so long/I've been lookin' for freedom/Still the search goes on' – it caught the mood of the nation and the album topped the charts for three months over the summer of 1989.

So on New Year's Eve 1989 – several weeks after the Wall was torn down – there was a certain loony kind of justice when Hasselhoff bestrode one of its remaining lumps to give a concert. As he sang 'Looking for Freedom', hundreds of thousands of ecstatic voices swelled beneath his. He – a man previously best-known for his performance with a talking car in *Knight Rider* – led the way to the Promised Land, armed only with a guitar and a cigarette lighter.

Perhaps it was his name: Germany may have mistaken him for a native. Or perhaps they had enjoyed his work in *The Young and the Restless*. That New Year's Eve, though, David Hasselhoff was swept up in the arms of history ... which must have been nice.

Over ten years later he gave an interview to a German magazine called *Spielfilm*, during which he mentioned his genuine disappointment that the Berlin Museum at Checkpoint Charlie had overlooked him in their exhibition on the fall of Communism. 'I find it a bit sad that there is no photo of me hanging on the walls in the museum', he was quoted as saying.

Now, this could be taken as evidence of a monstrous ego and was widely reported as such. The implication was that The Hoff believed that he had brought Communism staggering to its knees with a mere rustle of his leather trousers – although, in his defence, 'feeling a bit sad' isn't the most starry, hissy-fit-style response imaginable. He had been involved, certainly ... But, um, so were we all in some way or other (for instance, I mainly watched it on television). Rather than pulling off some Hollywood-style revolution through showbiz – in a reversal of cause and effect – it's far more

13

likely that a canny record industry executive had advised him to do a version of the song because, in their judgement, it would be in tune with the burgeoning mood of the nation.

I met David Hasselhoff once, at a party for the last performance of *Cats* in the West End of London. He was an unselfconsciously pleasant man in a long leather coat and he helpfully gave me a diary story for the paper that had sent me there. I admired his full head of hair, was slightly amazed to have met him and then forgot all about it until the next time someone made a 'Hoff' joke (a friend who's perennially pleased with a card she once received showing a naked Hasselhoff wearing only strategically placed puppies).

The man is an icon. He's famous mainly for his unashamedly populist work – who could forget *Baywatch* – and appears admirably unperturbed that his oeuvre may not stand the test of time. My feeling on the subject is very much: 'What's not to like?' You can be too judgemental …

A few hundred miles away on the edge of the Baltic, the artistic community of Vilnius in Lithuania was also profoundly affected by events atop the Berlin Wall in 1989. It experienced a blossoming after the fall of its own Communist regime that eventually, and rather bizarrely, manifested itself as a statue of Frank Zappa.

At four feet high, it's not a particularly large statue, although to its eternal credit it replaced another, less amusing one of Lenin that had stood nearby. Zappa is in bronze, cast by Konstantinas Bogdanus, a renowned Lithuanian sculptor who had previously made his entire living by producing portraits of that particular Communist leader.

The Zappa statue was willed into existence by a group of artists and friends who had discovered the unabashedly weird rock guitarist during the initial rush of access to American music, which had previously been suppressed. Frank Zappa was an emblem of freedom to them and they lunged at him with an inspired exuberance.

Their first attempt to spread the word to their 3 million fellow Lithuanians involved two bogus exhibits at a local art museum, one of which featured letters supposedly written by the great man to his Lithuanian admirers. The startled local reaction rapidly produced a second exhibit titled 'Memorial objects of Frank Zappa', including clocks, knives, pens and clothes, purportedly 'owned' by the musician. In fact, they all belonged to one of the artists, a man called Saulius Paukstys.

The artwork was a massive hit. On a roll, the Zappa fan club told local and national media that the work had been catalysed by an encounter that Paukstys had with the great man on a trip to the United States. While this was what everyone wanted to hear, it wasn't actually true.

A statue was proposed to the local city council, 300 signatures were collected, the artists said that they would raise the money themselves – which they did – and the statue of Zappa's ponytailed head was eventually raised in a park by the owner of a construction company, in exchange for a bottle of booze.

By all accounts, the opening ceremony was a triumph of Central European absurdism. A military orchestra played Zappa's tunes as fireworks exploded in the sky overhead – although since it was daylight their main effect was to fill the area with smoke so that it resembled a Meat Loaf video.

And all this was simply because they liked Frank Zappa, a man who named one of his children Moon Unit and whose fans have always celebrated the bizarre. The guitarist had no Lithuanian connection, he had never visited the country and none of the artists involved had ever met him. He was seized on with a kind of bonkers exhilaration as a symbol of events over which he had no control or, indeed, real involvement.

David Hasselhoff and Frank Zappa are two men who, as musicians, temporarily became more than the sum of their parts and collided slightly awkwardly with history. In a sense they are part of a tradition of popular entertainers whose names are associated with particular events – Vera Lynn springs to mind – because like a scent, music carries memories in an oblique way, separate from the intention of the parfumier or singer who created the original. It can be intensely personal but is also a shared public experience – splicing together a million personal historical moments.

When the Wall came down in November 1989, I was in Jerusalem as a volunteer for the Israeli ambulance service. I believe it was a Friday afternoon because the Sabbath starts at sundown, bringing an abrupt end to most things in that city, including the bus service.

## DID DAVID HASSELHOFF END THE COLD WAR?

My shift had run over and I remember rushing along Jaffa Street trying to get to a jazz club on Bezalel, where the volunteers would usually have a couple of beers before sprinting for the last bus.

I glanced down in my haste and saw a pile of copies of the *Jerusalem Post* – which was usually a morning paper – sitting on the pavement where they had just been unwrapped. 'Berlin Wall comes down' screamed the headline.

I was nineteen. I paid little attention and kept going, my mind on the beer to come. When I got to the club I sat down, ordered a Maccabee and said to some of my colleagues: 'You'll never guess what I just saw.' When I told them, they looked at me very strangely before getting up and leaving wordlessly to buy a newspaper.

Once back at the former ambulance station on the West Bank that served as a rackety old home for volunteers, we glued ourselves to the television. We watched images of people dancing on top of the Wall, many wearing party outfits of ra-ra skirts and military-looking items like peaked hats and jackets with brass buttons and epaulettes. Periodically, people gleefully knocked chunks out of the Wall.

All of us were British or American, rubbish at languages and we couldn't understand a word. The news was in Hebrew, which was no good to us, and on the other channel it was in Arabic, which was even less familiar. Underneath the images, when the commentary stopped, they played a cheesy song called 'The Winds of Change' by the Scorpions, an overblown rock anthem that had previously produced nothing in me except a vague feeling of indigestion. 'Take me, to the magic of the moment/On a glory night/Where the children of tomorrow dream away/In the wind of change.' That day it brought tears to my eyes and, whenever a snatch of it floats through the air in a shopping centre or from someone's car window, it still does.

# Europeans are genetically modified to consume more alcohol than the rest of the world

The continent of Europe has about 12.5 per cent of the world's population but consumes about 50 per cent of its alcoholic drinks. Some will suck their teeth, shake their heads and feel concerned about this because, as with many things, the topic of alcohol is usually raised in public only when it's a problem. Under-age and binge drinking, hooliganism, calorific nightmares, a social prop for inadequates, bringer-on of diseases, killer of children and drivers and a last redoubt for those hiding from themselves: the media anatomises the demon drink in these contexts on a daily basis.

However, alcohol can be many things to many people and not all of its purposes are malign. Imagine how many relationships would never have got off the ground without a little Dutch courage to tip introverts in the right direction, or how many children would not have been conceived without the enthusiasm that beer goggles can promote. And I still believe that getting quietly blotto after receiving bad news can help one over a crucial emotional hump.

All this and more is possible because, as a molecule, alcohol has the ability to mimic other substances including ether (an anaesthetic), amphetamine, valium and opium. An alcoholic drink can be stimulating, depressing and mood-altering in any number of different ways, depending on the other compounds giving it colour and flavour, and the context in which it's consumed.

Similarly, alcohol has an external geography that varies over time and space. Northern Europe has its notorious vodka belt of melancholy alcoholics, whose long, dark nights are populated by inner demons. This 'forces' the state to control drinking by price. Few Scandinavians keep alcohol in their homes, the legend goes, as they are mysteriously conditioned to finish a bottle of anything once it has been opened.

Southern Europe, by contrast, is stereotypically home to the moderate drinker of a convivial glass of red, consumed over slow

17

meals in the sunshine as part of a highly nutritious Mediterranean diet. In reality, the way most people use alcohol hovers somewhere between these two versions.

Alcohol is inextricably woven into the fabric of European societies: used to celebrate or commiserate and as a social lubricant, a symbol of adulthood or a 'punishment' in a drinking game. Frothing tankards of ale or mead are part of British folk mythology, usually served by buxom wenches in merrye tavernes. And there's a good reason for all this alcoholic nonsense ... beyond the fact that it can also be fun.

Matt Ridley, in his book *Genome*, says that most people have the capacity to pump up the production of substances called alcohol dehydrogenases, which allow the body to digest alcohol. This is a trick, he says, that we learnt the hard way over generations – by the deaths of people who could not do it.

The argument runs that when people began living in densely packed towns and cities in the Middle Ages, water quality became a real problem for the first time. Water-borne diseases like cholera and typhoid thrived where sewage and drinking water mingled, meaning that having ways to guard against these killers became crucial in order to survive into adulthood.

In much of Europe, people developed the habit of mixing water with alcohol in the form of wine or beer. Fermented liquids are relatively sterile, so those who used alcohol generally survived to have children, and those who didn't tended to die young of water-borne diseases. Hence a 'preference' for people with genes able to break down alcohol quickly became a part of the landscape.

These days, 'don't drink the water' is almost a European superstition, offered most frequently to those off travelling in exotic climes. But we easily forget that until recently we didn't even drink our own water – and with good reason.

In the summer of 1854, Soho in London was an insanitary place, full of cowsheds, animal droppings, slaughterhouses, grease-boiling dens and primitive, decaying sewers. Underneath the floorboards of its overcrowded cellars lurked a sea of cesspits, many as old as the houses above them and plenty that had never been drained. They were a bacteriological time-bomb.

The previous year, 10,675 people had died of cholera in London, and in August 1854 it was Soho's turn. In just three days, 127 people were killed. Within a week, three-quarters of the population had fled the area, leaving only the poorest behind. By that time the death toll had risen to 500.

Among the terrified population was a man called Dr John Snow, an anaesthesiologist who rapidly became a pioneer in epidemiology. He interviewed the families of the dead and dying in an attempt to isolate the source of infection. Despite the popular misconception that it was spread by a 'miasma in the atmosphere', Dr Snow believed that it was probably water-borne.

His investigations took him to a pump on the corner of Broad Street and Cambridge Street. On examining a water sample under his new-fangled microscope, he was convinced that the 'white, flocculent particles' he saw were the cholera bacterium. He went to the Board of Guardians of St James's parish, in which the Soho outbreak had occurred, and persuaded them to remove the pump handle. Shortly afterwards the outbreak ended – but only after 616 people had been killed.

Part of the puzzle that led Dr Snow to the pump was the 70 workers of a brewery on Broad Street, who had a daily allowance of beer and therefore no reason to drink the local water. None of them had contracted cholera, making them a microcosm of the selection that scientists now suggest took place Europe-wide over hundreds of years.

Many thousands of Europeans down through the centuries have had alcohol to thank for their personal survival – which is certainly worth a toast – and their genes live on to tell the tale. In much of the rest of the world, though, the preferred method for sterilising drinking water involved boiling it up with tea. Although alcohol was available, for instance as sake in Japan, it was not crucial to possess the gene to break it down because tea provided a popular life-saving alternative. So we see the phenomenon known as 'Asian blush', in which drinkers get drunk comparatively quickly and their faces light up like electric beetroots. In about half of all east Asians the relevant enzyme – aldehyde dehydrogenase – doesn't work as effectively as it does in most Europeans, and as a result there's good reason to pity the quality of their hangovers.

Similarly, traditional hunter-gatherers like Native Americans,

Aboriginal Australians and Greenland Inuits never needed such a gene, since their population densities were not great enough to make clean water a problem. It's no coincidence that all three have a reputation for being bad with booze.

To tell this as a story about natural selection – pointing to the teetotallers who didn't survive, and our mildly-alcoholic ancestors who did – hopefully makes it readily understandable. But there are also scientists who feel that this version of events is painfully over-simplified. They argue that it puts the 'engine' of evolution in the wrong place, giving a man-made narrative that is inappropriate to the point of being wrong.

Instead, they point out that at a molecular level a certain number of spontaneous mutations occur within any period of time and that the ability to break down alcohol was only one of these. It's these predictable mutations that make it possible for us to measure the number of years that have elapsed since the family tree of our human ancestors diverged from that of other species.

Many bacteria also have the enzyme aldehyde dehydrogenase, so it's probably our common ancestry with these single-cell organisms that accounts for the presence of the enzyme in the human body. It allows us to produce and break down lactic acid (an alcohol produced by muscle) when we run, as well as to recover from drinking alcohol instead of being poisoned by it. After all, it would be no good trying to escape from a sabre-toothed tiger if lactic acid paralysed your muscles after only a few yards. Aldehyde dehydrogenase, scientists argue, has been the key to survival at many other points during our genetic history apart from when humans started living in filthy towns.

We can't know for sure all the ways in which alcohol and its associated enzymes have helped us over the years – the story being as much about the telling as the tale. But ultimately, the unusual European affinity for alcohol came about because we have been able to use it as more than just an interesting drink.

# There are half a million semi-automatic machine guns in Swiss homes

Switzerland has an undeserved reputation for being dull, thanks to Orson Welles. In *The Third Man*, in an off-the-cuff addition to the Graham Greene script, he said: 'In Italy for 30 years under the Borgias they had warfare, terror, murder and bloodshed – they produced Michelangelo, Leonardo da Vinci and the Renaissance. In Switzerland they had brotherly love and 500 years of democracy and peace and what did they produce? The cuckoo clock.'

With all due respect to Orson Welles (as people often remark before saying something disrespectful), the cuckoo clock was invented by Franz Kellerer in the Black Forest, which is definitely in Germany. Moreover, every Swiss border represents a real and bloody battle that took place between Switzerland and a neighbour at some point in the past.

The place has no 'natural' borders at all, because the Alps simply continue on into Austria, Germany, France and Italy. It's hard, especially from a British perspective, to imagine what this might mean for a country's personality.

In Switzerland, people speak French, German and Italian: there is no such tongue as 'Swiss'. So in the absence of clearly-defined linguistic or geographic edges to their culture, they scrutinise anything that looks like it might be uniquely Swiss for clues about who they, the Swiss, might be. This national journey of self-discovery is aided at a local level by the existence of cantons and communities in which referendums are a way of life.

Jonathan Steinberg, in his book *Why Switzerland?*, suggests that the country's precarious mountainous position has produced a split personality in its people. They enjoy the highest standard of living in the world, but suffer paranoia and anxiety because their wealth makes them feel abnormal in comparison with their neighbours. It is hard not to take a certain amount of satisfaction in this.

He writes about a *Sonderfall Schweiz* – 'a Swiss special case, which emerged from the fusion of geographic factors … the physical strength of the mountaineers, the accumulation of urban wealth, neutrality, the peculiar religious mosaic, the use of direct democratic devices, federalism, communal autonomy, multilingualism and those unwritten rules of behaviour which lead to … conflict avoidance and tolerance'.

But all this harmony and wealth comes at its own price. Twelve per cent of the population who die before the age of 72 commit suicide, and Switzerland has the highest incidence of Aids in western Europe – although the medical authorities would argue that they are simply better informed about what's going on in their country than most.

Switzerland was the first place in the world to make catalytic converters compulsory on cars, yet it's a nation of heavy smokers – around 30 per cent of the population puff, 20 per cent have recently given up, and you rarely find a Swiss restaurant with a non-smoking section.

In fact, air is a bit of a national obsession. The curiously large number of Swiss nuclear fallout shelters are referred to as 'air protection shelters', as if air would be the only important issue in the event of a nuclear explosion. There is also a warm wind that blows in off the Mediterranean, known locally as the *Föhn*, meaning hairdryer in German. When it gusts up over the Alps it causes headaches, the suicide rate is driven up even further, befuddled car drivers have apparently unprovoked accidents and the Swiss basically go crazy. The country regards this unregulated movement of air as catastrophically disruptive and unwelcome.

There is a similar national feeling about 'foreigners'. Although 20 per cent of Switzerland's 7.3 million residents are classified as 'non-citizens', more than half of them have lived in the country for more than fifteen years. The 'foreigners' have more children than the Swiss – they represent 26.5 per cent of the country's new-borns – and while 50,231 *Ausländers* arrived in 2002, 2,576 Swiss citizens emigrated.

Switzerland has also remained outside the European Union – why join a poor man's club? And it has hung on to its historic position of 'neutrality', although since Austria joined the EU in 1995, it has been completely surrounded by EU members.

This is quite odd when you think about it. In most circumstances, being encircled by an empire of which one isn't a member would be profoundly unsettling. In fact, since the Swiss are discombobulated by a strong breeze, it probably *is* disturbing for them. Otherwise it's hard to explain why the country maintains a citizens' army or militia of half a million people – armed to the teeth with all kinds of heavy weaponry, including grenades and rocket launchers – ready for swift mobilisation in the event of an invasion ... by the Italians?

All male Swiss citizens – but none of the country's 'foreigners' – are required by the constitution to register for national service, and women can volunteer if they are feeling belligerent or helpful. The number of years one remains 'in service' was recently reduced from 30 to 22. National service involves several months' training, followed by regular manoeuvres and retraining courses, while maintaining one's weapon at home in a constant state of readiness: it is an old-fashioned citizens' militia, similar to the Israeli Defence Force, or American soldiers during the War of Independence.

It isn't unusual to see a farmer pedalling over the mountain on a bicycle (although the Swiss army recently disbanded its famous 'bicycle troop') with an automatic rifle slung over his back, off to target practice.

'The quality of the StGW 57 rifle's manufacture is excellent', said David Fortier, who reviews weapons for *Guns* magazine. 'It's beautifully made, though being typically Swiss, it is also overly complex. It is machined from high-quality materials but it's heavy at 13.5 pounds and somewhat awkward.'

'You wouldn't be able to use it in a close-quarter battle – it's too unwieldy. But it would have been useful for trying to bump off Soviet invaders as they came over the mountains, before they were close enough to bring their overwhelming firepower to bear. In reserve hands it would be a fine weapon for practising basic marksmanship and for competition at 100, 300 and 600 metres.'

As of March 2005, there were 200,723 beautifully manufactured killing machines bristling in Swiss wardrobes, which is an awful lot of guns for such a small country. There were also 156,100 of a slightly more modern version, which Mr Fortier reckons is 'overrated on account of it being Swiss'. But then he is an American.

Yet no one can remember the last time that a Swiss assault rifle was fired against an invader. Hitler never got around to Switzerland

– presumably he didn't want to annoy them while his loot was stashed in Zurich banks. In fact, 1604 was the last time Switzerland was called upon to repel a foreign invader, and the semi-automatic was not, at that time, the weapon of choice.

Niccolò dei Machiavelli once said: 'Gli Svizzeri sono armatissimi et liberissimi.' – 'The Swiss are the most armed and the most free.' As if in tribute, the Vatican has used Swiss guards for the Pope's personal protection since 1506. Perhaps miraculously, they too haven't had to fight anyone since 1527.

Journalists at one of Reuters' two Swiss bureaux could remember only two crimes involving guns in recent decades: one involving a man in a latex suit who was shot by his girlfriend, and a spree at the national parliament – each was especially memorable in its own way.

The available Swiss crime statistics don't break down how many killings happened with guns and how many with alpine horns or heavy-duty cow bells – but one suspects that if guns were a problem, the police would have a dedicated taskforce, as they do in London, where guns are illegal. Everyone at the news agency and the Swiss Embassy in London was in agreement that very few killings, with guns or otherwise, take place in Switzerland.

What's hard to know or understand in all this, is whether it's safe for the Swiss to have so many weapons because they are a civilised and peaceable nation – or whether they are peaceable because historically they have been so well-defended? Whichever it is, it seems to work for them.

Switzerland doesn't want to join the European Union … or anything else. (They are also surrounded by members of the North Atlantic Treaty Organization (NATO) although they show no inclination to join that group either.) And while they continue to spend their evenings up in the mountains polishing their rifles, it's unlikely that anyone will seek seriously to persuade them to do so.

# Albania is the worst place in Europe

Very little is ever written about Albania and there are some good reasons for this. Norman Wisdom, the comic actor, is to this day a huge celebrity there and this snippet of bizarre pub trivia suffices to confirm to cosmopolitan Brits that the place is a bit unusual. But very few, having digested this fascinating fact, then summon the curiosity to visit. Indeed, the British Foreign and Commonwealth Office's travel website advises that it's dangerous to journey outside the capital, Tirana.

The place's best-known export is 'gangsterism'. In particular, Albanians have seized control of much of the heroin traffic throughout western Europe since 1991. Albanian-run people-trafficking is also rife, with the country serving both as a place of origin and transit. Save the Children recently estimated that 60 per cent of those trafficked from Albania are children, sold mainly for prostitution.

This trade is self-destructive on a national scale, for a European country in which 30 per cent of the population live below the poverty line, and 15 per cent struggle on less than a dollar a day. And this in a country that shares a border with Greece and has the heel of Italy only a few miles across the water. The average annual per capita income in Albania was £1,740 in 2003. In Europe, only Bosnia-Herzegovina had a lower average income – but since Bosnia is rapidly recovering from a civil war, this is unlikely to be the case for long.

Enver Hoxha was Albania's Stalinist dictator for 40 years until his death in 1985, and he kept the place in a state of complete isolation from the outside world. One of my favourite Albania stories is how, in order to maintain this isolation, Hoxha built around half a million one-man concrete pillboxes, or gun turrets, along the country's borders. He told his people that the quality of their lives was so high in comparison with the rest of the world, that the turrets were needed to prevent hordes of marauding Westerners bursting over their borders. After the final fall of the regime in 1991, some brave Albanians stumbled up to the mountainous borders and noticed that all the slits on the gun turrets were pointing inwards.

25

Such isolation has had extremely unfortunate effects on a country that is already riven by a culture of blood feuds that makes Sicily look like a model of state-run order. During the 1920s the death-rate for young Albanian men ran to 20 per cent a year – and this was in the absence of a civil war.

In 1997, the official annual murder rate in Albania was 76.9 people per 100,000. Compare this with the most recent equivalent figures from Interpol: in the United Kingdom in 2001 the murder rate was 1.63 per 100,000 people, and in France in 2000 it was 3.7 per 100,000. Based on these figures, the chances of getting murdered in Albania were about 50 times higher than they were in Britain, or twenty times higher than they were in France for those years.

And that is if you are an Albanian. A foreign passport is worth around £3,500 on the black market. This makes foreigners and their worldly goods of considerable interest to an impoverished population that has one of the highest emigration rates in the world. Over 1991 and 1992, 300,000 people left the country, with a similar number departing over the subsequent four years. Then there was another peak over 1996 and 1997, when some government-run pyramid schemes collapsed – yes, the government actually ran pyramid schemes – and 70,000 more decided to seek their fortunes elsewhere. In total, 35 per cent of the population has emigrated since 1991, and there were only around 3 million Albanians in the first place.

So travelling to Albania can be a bit of a risky business. Robert Carver, a journalist and film-maker, is one of the few people to have done so and written about it. Although there are a handful of other travel guides, his is the only discursive English volume written since the Second World War that is readily available from Amazon.

*The Accursed Mountains* was published in 1999 to some acclaim. Carver describes the emotional arc of his journey through Albania. He begins optimistically with tales from Anglo-Albanian friendship societies in London about the quality of Albanian hospitality, and from a Greek taxi driver who, on the way to the border, described the place as being just like Greece after the civil war: 'No cars, much poverty, broken houses, donkeys and mules, no work – but … a sweetness.'

Within a relatively short period, though, the author's feelings of optimism apparently drain away, sapped by the Albanians he encounters. After being severely ripped off over a fish dinner by people who were supposed to be helping him, he announces: 'I had been told fairy stories about Albanian honesty and trust, about looking after the foreign guest. These people were crooks who lied and fawned on you for advantage, and then cheated you when they had lulled you into believing their lies ...'

'I had begun to recognise that Albanians never offered information to one another, never helped each other, except for favours of money. Everyone strove to get the better of the other by cheating or stealing. Duplicity and trickery were the currency of everyday life: the cunning man, the successful cheat or swindler, was greatly admired. Honesty, frankness, fair trading were all despised as naïve. Cynicism was intelligence, fairness stupidity.'

Although he meets the odd friendly soul and has a lot of nice things to say about the scenery, the overwhelming impression is of a place fundamentally flawed by its allegiance to tribal family groupings called *fis*, and impaled on the attitudes that arise from it. He writes:

'What could you say about a culture where outside the *fis* everyone stole and was proud of it; where girls were kidnapped at fifteen and sold into prostitution; where lying was normal and the government stole more than anyone else? Where people trafficked in guns, drugs and false identity papers, and went to richer countries deliberately to rob and pillage? Where wife-beating was normal, rape and buggery the fate meted out to anyone not protected by either guns or their family? Where sadistic torture by secret police is routine and everything from a school certificate to a doctor's degree could be bought for cash? Where the blood feud and revenge killings paralysed whole swathes of the land, drenching them in the gore of innocent children of seven or eight.'

'And you read the cleaned-up version', Carver told me over the telephone. 'The publisher took out a whole load of stuff because the original draft was so negative! It is a very strange place and it attracts very strange people. There are three separate Anglo-Albanian societies in Britain and none of them will talk to each other.'

He went on to explain: 'One of the troubles with trying to get to

DID DAVID HASSELHOFF END THE COLD WAR?

grips with it, is that it is really too dangerous to go swanning around as an independent traveller, so you have to attach yourself to some *fis* or other, simply in order to gain protection against the others. But then outsiders get a kind of tourist version of Stockholm Syndrome, where they get drawn into the feuding. Anybody who gets involved with Albania gets into blood feuds. I haven't had anything to do with the place since I left precisely for that reason. It's just too dangerous.'

He mentioned an incident in June 1997, in which food aid was being distributed by a Greek Orthodox charity in the south of the country under the protection of the Italian army. While the food was being handed out, Albanian snipers fired on the soldiers, aid workers and the recipients because the aid was going to a rival *fis*. In Albania, anyone helping one's enemies is also an enemy.

'But people in Europe can't believe it when you tell them about things like this. They can't believe it. To which my response is: go there yourself if you don't believe me and look for yourself. I have never been anywhere worse than Albania and couldn't wait to get out of the place. It was awful.'

And since so many Albanians apparently feel the same way, it's hard to argue.

# The EU has a special gift for making things seem boring

It is a truth universally acknowledged that Europe is a dull subject.

Who among us has never realised, after a few minutes of staring dumbly at a television screen, that they can't recall a crumb of the news item explaining the intricacies of the latest round of EU trade talks, that the jousting over the Common Agricultural Policy has made them feel hungry, or that some court case involving Turkey and human rights has provoked an urgent need for a pee?

It's as if a veil of tedium settles over one's brain in such a way that information about the European Union glances off it, sheering away without making any impression. Off it cruises ... perhaps reassembling as some kind of weather pattern over Brussels: 'The temperature on the ground is a stable 19 degrees Celsius and the outlook is probably something to do with milk subsidies.' Dull.

In 2005, the Belgian arm of the European Commission released a children's book called *L'Europe mon Foyer*, or *Europe: My Home*. In it, two young friends, Lea and Thomas, find themselves accosted by a flying dwarf (as you do) called Papa Houpette, who takes them on a skyline tour of the Continent. Along the way he explains the basics of the European Union, beginning with a description and picture of the flag.

It's the dullest children's book you are ever likely to come across, combining pomposity, didacticism and the mundane in such a way that after a few pages, it's more entertaining to colour in the pictures (which I did) than to continue reading.

How is it possible, you may well ask, that a flying dwarf can be made to seem boring? Two child-friendly ideas – a convivial dwarf and flying – have been combined for the purposes of entertainment. What could possibly go wrong? If the worst came to the worst, surely the authors could have fallen back on tried and tested ideas? Papa Houpette could have arrived on a scarlet bicycle to cast a special EU spell. 'Subsidiarmus!' he may well have squeaked, flicking his magical metric ruler in the direction of Peter Mandelson and turning him into a sack of something nice.

But no. The curse of the EU strikes again. Instead of being told anything interesting, amusing or useful about Europe (our home, lest we forget), we find out from Papa Houpette that all the EU missions have their own internet sites, that Jean Monnet and Robert Schuman – the evil twins of European bureaucratic history – existed (yes!), and that so far there have been five phases of the European Union's development. Stunning, eh?

As with Papa Houpette, so with the news. Over and over again, the media tells us stories about the EU's shape and process instead of describing the relationship between the organisation and people's lives. Why should people hear anything about Europe's blood feuds, dungeons, piracy, food, gods or monsters, when instead they can receive accounts of important trade talks with insufficient context to make sense of them, or of wrangling over who gets which of the Commission's portfolios?

Machiavelli is alive and well and causing people to fall off the tops of tall buildings in Brussels (Chapter 47 is dedicated to poor old Antonio Quatraro). But why focus on that, when instead it's possible to spend hours pointing out once again that the Common Agricultural Policy appears to be designed solely for the edification of French businessmen who like to keep three or four chickens at their weekend home in the country?

These dull things are means to an end, not ends in themselves, yet they're all we really know about the European Union: our home. It's like telling the news in Britain by reading out the minutes of House of Commons committee meetings – as a result, it's not surprising that 'EU' and 'boring' go together like boats and seasickness.

After a while the accumulation of threadbare trivia takes on a life of its own – it diverts attention away from itself by carrying the implicit message: 'If you want to know anything fascinating, look away now.'

The same was true at college. As a politics student, I did a course on European government that was remarkable only for its mind-numbing qualities. Revising for the exam was the only time I ever fell asleep with my head on a book and I noticed later, as I was trying to lift my head from the table, that the stain of several other peoples' saliva graced the same page on which I'd been attempting to focus. The shade of Robert Schuman lurked malevolently around the library stack to bore me into submission by telling me about subsidiarity, and I couldn't work out at the time why the tutor who taught the course was never seen around the department and didn't appear to teach any other courses.

The 'Europe' course was a cul-de-sac, apparently unrelated to anything else, taught by a man who had specialised himself into indispensability. But that was all over a decade ago and it's possible that a quiet revolution in thinking about the subject may have taken place since then.

Why do so many people think that Europe is a dull subject?, I enquired of several European studies professors.

Unfortunately, of the five I contacted, only one was sufficiently interested in the question to respond. 'The reason for that ennui (and the electoral apathy that meets European Parliament elections)', wrote Dr Roberto Espindola of the University of Bradford, 'in the decline on contestation that goes hand in hand with integration. Hope that helps.'

It didn't. I was pretty sure that he meant '*is* the decline *in* contestation', but even that didn't shed much light on anything. Also, 'contestation' is too little-used a word for such a simple concept: it means competition for something. Perplexed and a little annoyed, I wrote back. 'Sorry. I don't follow. Decline on contestation? Contestation of what? What do you mean?'

'My fault. Problems of writing quick email messages', he responded. 'I meant "in" contestation, not "on".'

I include this exchange because it bears the exact flavour of my course in European politics back in the 20th century. It was baffling, jargon-filled and ultimately pointless. I learned nothing from it worth knowing, and wished afterwards that I hadn't bothered – it was off-putting.

And this is a process that feeds on itself. If something is boring, dull people are attracted to it. If it can't be adequately explained, because tedium prevents us from arriving at a satisfying conclusion, then one will be disinclined to raise the topic again. Through sleight of hand, public attention on all matters political and European has been diverted.

Misdirection is the name for it. Show a European bureaucrat a beautiful forest, groaning with Europe's history of robbers and partisans, filled with the continent's last remaining herd of majestic bison (see Chapter 9), and they'd be inclined to tell you that there were several interesting specimens in there – some of them with leaves. Oh, yes. They can't see the wood for the trees or, at least, can't see the point in telling you anything interesting about the wood – and that's the way that their political masters would like it to stay.

The EU was created by governments that were themselves democratically elected, yet there's much about the organisation that is unresponsive to democratic pressures. If, over the years, we'd focused on it at too great a length, we might have become more uncomfortable with this burgeoning and expensive new form of government than we actually did, whatever its long-term advantages – you don't have to be a conspiracy theorist to see the logic of this. So the political miracle of its dullness has kept our attention safely ensconced on the football instead, or preoccupied by other matters closer to home.

The meaning of the EU buzz-word 'subsidiarity' was pretty much the only thing I learnt about Europe as a student that had any heft to it. It was a long word, I got the hang of it, I was young and I believed that one day it would come in handy ... Well, this is its big moment: within EU bureaucracy, it means the passing down of responsibility for the execution of policy to the lowest practical level.

It wasn't until years later that someone pointed out to me that, in order for the idea to make sense, one had to accept the premise that all the power referred to within the concept of subsidiarity lived at the top of the organisation in the first place. And that this was not remotely democratic ... It had taken me ten years to cotton on.

Only by retaining their magical powers of misdirection-through-boredom will the European Union's legions of flying dwarves be able to continue to baffle us into paying very little attention to what they're doing. The odds are on their side, though – they've been successful for the last 60 years.

# The EU's border between Poland and Belarus divides a primeval forest where wolves, lynx, and bison with the clap roam

The forest of Bialowieza in Poland, which is called Belovezhskaya in Belarus, is on the EU's outside edge. It sits on the border, unevenly distributed between the two countries – with about 40 per cent in Poland – and is so old that it suggests to visitors intoxicated by its scale that nothing ever really changes. There be dragons! At least, it wouldn't be entirely surprising if there were …

Poland joined the EU in 2004, but Belarus is, at the time of writing, governed by Alexander Lukashenko, a Soviet-style throwback of a dictator who once ordered his military to shoot down two American balloonists when they drifted across his territory during an international race. On another occasion, in July 1998, he welded the American ambassador's gate shut, when foreign diplomats in the capital Minsk refused to leave their homes on his orders. As a result he has been barred from ever entering the United States, the European Union or Japan.

The forest on the border is reckoned to be around 10,000 years old and is often referred to as 'primeval'– it once blanketed Europe from the Atlantic to the Urals. Ancient oak, ash, linden, hornbeam and maple trees grow to vast sizes there, sometimes for several centuries. Often, when they fall, they are left lying to feed fungi and termites, filling the air with a musk of decay. The forest glistens with mosses and mushrooms, and thin pale violets and broad redcaps dot the forest floor, while above nest rare birds, including the three-toed woodpecker.

The ecosystem is a valuable scientific resource and there are institutes on both sides of the border dedicated to researching its intricacies. But people also sense something distinctly unscientific about the place: it provokes romance because its smells and sounds would have been familiar to the early men and women of northern Europe. It elicits a form of ancestor worship.

Forests like this lie at the heart of European mythology. They have sheltered partisans and revolutionaries, many of whom now lie beneath the forest floor, and are the terra incognita where Hansel and Gretel almost lost their lives to a witch and Little Red Riding Hood was menaced by a wolf. Goblin and faerie hordes have poured from its hollows, and legend has it that, in this particular place, blue-blooded, green-whiskered wood fauns known as *Leshy* lead their enemies astray.

It's also the last redoubt of Europe's largest land animal: the wild bison, or *Bison bonasus*. The species, although once extinct in the wild (shot by hungry German soldiers in 1919) has been cleverly resurrected by a breeding programme using animals from zoos in Germany and Scandinavia. The story of the bison is emblematic of a disagreement about the essential nature of the forest.

Appropriately enough, there is not one herd of the rare creatures, but two. They are divided by a tall metal fence along the border and the road running alongside it is patrolled by guards on sputtering motorbikes: this is the EU's hinterland, suggesting its Cold War past.

On the Polish side, 17 per cent of the forest is a national park, as is the whole of the Belorussian forest. But the term 'national park' has several different definitions, according to the International Union for the Conservation of Nature. On the Belorussian side, many families live and work there and even hunting is still permitted. But in Poland, the forest's national park status has meant that a lot of people – and disproportionately the young – have had to leave to find work elsewhere.

Traditionally, there have been many ways to live in the forest: bee-keeping, charcoal production, animal-breeding, hay meadows, game-keeping, poaching, mushroom- and berry-picking, the stripping of bark from trees for shoe-making and tannin. The woodland economy has supported people as economies do anywhere else.

But Bialowieza has also become a cause célèbre for ecologists, environmentalists and scientists in recent years. By describing it as 'primeval', they have suggested to an international internet community that the area is somehow less touched by human influence than other places – more 'natural' – and have garnered support for turning more of the Polish forest into a national park. Ideally, their thinking goes, this would be a 'peace park' along the lines of the cross-border tracts in Africa, which were created for large carnivorous mammals whose hunting grounds were artificially divided by nation-state borders.

In 2000, there were demonstrations in places as far away as Canada and Geneva in favour of 'saving' the forest in Poland (few believed that Lukashenko would be susceptible to their pleading) from the malign influence of people and their tendency towards activities like logging. Instead the environmentalists wanted to turn it over to the wild boar, bison and 170 or so species of bird that nest there.

But 800 local people, whose livelihoods depended on it, had a demonstration of their own, during which the Polish Minister for the Environment was pelted with eggs. The Polish government – which since the early 1990s has, after all, relied on Poles to vote for it – wound back its own plans to extend the national park shortly afterwards.

'It is a working landscape', said Stuart Franklin, a geographer from Oxford University and photographer, who spent a year and a half living and researching in Bialowieza.

'The only difference between the shoe-makers of the past and the area's new entrepreneurs is that whereas before people made things, now a lot of the scientific community are getting grants on the basis of the myth of pristinity. But it's just another economic niche. The scientific community is filling another niche in the forest in the same way that the mushroom-gatherers did. We all look for a niche.'

He argues that the forest landscape is inseparable from the political geography of the area, and that to try to divide the trees from the people who live with and from them is artificial. Yet because we receive abstracted environmental concerns from the internet – and what else does the internet ever do except abstract our reality? – we miss out on crucial information.

'Those who live in Bialowieza are fed up with people from Geneva or Brussels telling them what they should or shouldn't do. Logging has become a pejorative term, although there is nothing wrong with cutting down trees in the context of managing the forest. The problems arise, in fact, when you don't, because old trees get diseased. City people tend to think that old trees are great. But young trees, saplings can be great too. The survival of the forest ultimately depends on them.'

'The issue of enlarging the national park was a war that took place on the internet, conducted by scientists and environmentalists – and they very nearly won. But what was really at stake was access and money. The people living around the forest on both sides of the border have very little of either. Some people in the world have access to the internet and quite often democracy becomes skewed by people's access to information and their ability to disseminate information. This is the heartland of political ecology.'

Pity the bison then, caught up in an internet debate but really with far more pressing concerns. These days there are around 300 of them, but they are not very well and are being selectively culled like so many forest dwellers before them. Not to put it too delicately: their testicles are dropping off.

The breeding programme which resurrected them brought together a small number of the bison – or *wisent* as they are known locally – from zoos around the world. But one of the male animals did most of the, erm, work and as a result all the bison in Bialowieza have the same Y-chromosome. This has made the male animals susceptible to a serious infection of the genitalia called necrotising balanoposthitis that, unfortunately, makes their testicles fall off, with obvious implications for the herd's long-term viability. Attempts to cull the problem out of existence have not worked.

The bison, like the forest, is a national icon for both Poland and Belarus. There are three beers and even a bank named after the enormous animals, which, at sometimes nearly seven feet high, are Europe's largest land mammal. So when the national beast of two nations comes down with something like the clap, it's a bad blow to regional morale. That the problem is partly man-made is symptomatic of much else that goes on around Bialowieza.

# The average Papua New Guinean is more intelligent than the average European

At least, so argues Dr Jared Diamond, in his acclaimed book *Guns, Germs and Steel*. This work of anthropology covers about 13,000 years of human history, attempting to answer the question: why did Europe develop in such a way that its inhabitants explored and then conquered most of the rest of the world, rather than the other way around? It won the Rhone-Poulenc Science Prize in 1998.

Dr Diamond's argument about Europeans versus Papua New Guineans is firstly a Darwinian one. The environment in New Guinea, he says, still selects for intelligence, in the sense that the main causes of death there are murder, chronic tribal warfare, accidents and problems finding food. A person has to be of above-average intelligence to survive into adulthood.

By contrast, all Europeans have to do to transmit their genes is survive childhood diseases and have sex – and surviving diseases has become immensely easier with the advent of inoculation. It still helps if one's parents have the wit to, for instance, recognise a meningitis rash when they see one, so intelligence still has some hereditary component. But natural selection is at its rawest when the 'unfit' are removed from the gene pool before they can breed – and most Europeans survive into old age.

A second prong to his argument is that Europeans and Westerners generally are entertained as children in a largely passive way – through the media. Television, radio and movies make idiots of us all, he suggests, producing generation after generation of mentally stunted individuals, who have lost their initiative through spending seven hours a day in front of a TV.

New Guineans, on the other hand, spend their childhoods interacting with other children and adults. Since, Dr Diamond says, almost all studies of child development emphasise the role of childhood stimulation and activity in promoting mental development, this 'contributes a non-genetic component to the superior mental function displayed by New Guineans'.

## DID DAVID HASSELHOFF END THE COLD WAR?

Dr Marilyn Strathern, from the anthropology department of Cambridge University, is also an expert on Papua New Guinea, but she has a different take on Dr Diamond's proposition. She argues that the role of technology in European society has produced a people who are used to having their needs anticipated. 'My computer decides that it knows what I want, so I don't have to understand how it works, or even choose many of my own actions', she said – reminding me of the annoying animated paperclip that tries to help you write letters, when you never had any trouble writing them with a pen.

'And when I come back from the supermarket, I simply have to put the ready-made meals in the fridge rather than thinking about the way that I am going to combine my ingredients. But Papua New Guineans don't have the advantages or carry the burden of 4,000 years of technology. When they look at a car they don't see something with technological weight, they see something to be dealt with and as a result generally have no problem tackling car repairs.'

In other words, a society that takes technology for granted is also a society that expects someone else to build and repair things: with our advanced technology comes technophobia.

But Dr Strathern takes issue with the assumption linking passive entertainment and intelligence. 'Listening to Western children talking about adverts on television is like listening to a cultural critique. They are aware of several different levels of reality, of the quality of the performances and the message that they are supposed to be receiving', she said.

'Papua New Guineans are much more concerned with sorting out their relationships with one another, and that knowledge is a means to an end, because they have to know about other people and what their intentions are' – always a help if you want to avoid being murdered.

Personally, I also have trouble with Dr Diamond's views about television. As the child of a television producer, I don't think that my sister or I watched television in a particularly passive way, since it was part of our family's livelihoods. Television was something to be thought about, analysed, deconstructed and engaged with over the dinner table. It was another topic of conversation. Although this is an extreme example, it illustrates that your relationship with TV isn't necessarily pre-determined – there are many ways that you can use the medium. And anyway, is there something that makes television fundamentally different from reading a book?

One of the things TV has made far easier is introducing modern humans to the stories of countless others, who come from different places and historical periods. As the viewer responds to their concerns, motivations and anxieties, each dollop of empathy adds a new tile to their internal mosaic. Without *Enemy at the Gate*, why would we ever consider what it would have been like to be a sniper in Stalingrad during the Second World War? Without *Mutiny on the Bounty*, why would we think about discipline in His Majesty's 18th-century navy? And without *Finding Nemo*, how would we realise that fish are people too?

Perhaps the passivity that Dr Diamond sees when he looks at Western children is actually a mechanism making it possible for unprecedentedly large numbers of people to live in a relatively small space without murdering each other as the New Guineans do? After all, what's the joy in being clever if your not-so-bright friends and family members have been killed? And why would you venerate a society that has violent death as a defining characteristic, even if the individuals who live in it are quite sharp?

There is a growing belief that technology is slowing the rate of human evolution by turning the world into one global village, and that evolution is already at a near standstill in Europe and America. As Professor Steve Jones said in his book, *The Language of the Genes*, the invention of the bicycle was the most significant event in the history of evolution – people finally had a serious choice about whether to marry their cousins or to pedal off to the next village in search of more attractive pickings.

Mutations are the building blocks of human evolution and frequently need to be reinforced by an identical mutation to become a real physical characteristic. So evolution happens much faster in small, isolated communities, where everyone has similar genes that are constantly being shuffled among the generations. In a stew of inbreeding, the useful mutant gene is far more likely to meet its match and be reproduced.

Conversely, in cities and places where international travel is normal, people often choose partners to whom they are unrelated.

Outbreeding produces healthier individuals, but also means that recessive mutations that traditionally led to evolution are constantly dominated by genes that represent the status quo. Given a choice, people are more attracted to something that they see as 'normal', minimising the chance that their children will have mutant characteristics.

So in a world where internet dating isn't unusual, we are just one large gene pool that will remain evolutionarily stagnant for the foreseeable future ... which isn't to say that Europeans (and Westerners generally) have entirely abandoned an attachment to 'survival of the fittest'.

The Darwin Awards make terrific reading for the black of heart, and can be found on the internet. They were invented 'to salute the improvement of the human genome by honouring those who accidentally kill themselves in really stupid ways'. Of course, 'of necessity, this honour is generally bestowed posthumously'.

Larry Walters, a truck driver from Los Angeles, was one of the rare exceptions. Known forever now as 'Lawn Chair Larry', he had always wanted to be able to fly. In 1982 he bought 45 weather balloons, filled them with helium and attached them to his favourite lawn chair, along with some sandwiches, soft drinks and a pellet gun. He had anticipated a gentle rise to about 30 feet in the air, where he planned to float around for a while before bringing himself down by bursting some of the balloons.

So it was a shock to him when, once untethered, his flying machine streaked across the LA skyline. It levelled off at 16,000 feet in the main approach to Los Angeles International airport – and stayed there for two hours. When Larry finally found the courage to use the pellet gun, he came down on a power line – blacking out a neighbourhood in Long Beach for twenty minutes – before being rescued. When a reporter asked why he'd done it, he replied: 'A man can't just sit around.' Eleven years later, unmarried and childless, the Vietnam veteran committed suicide by shooting himself in the heart. But he got an obituary in the *Los Angeles Times*.

Every society – European, New Guinean, you name it – has its fair share of idiots.

# In 2001, a brothel for women opened on the Swiss-German border

In a little town called Leibstadt on the Swiss side of the line, a hotel and bar calling itself Angels opened wide its doors for a new kind of business in December 2001. It was a variation on a theme, in the sense that brothels were – indeed are – legal in Switzerland. But hitherto there had been none catering for straight women, and this one was celebrated for a short while as the first of its kind in Europe.

Five male prostitutes were installed and a titillated media provided free advertising for the bordello, which was housed in a typical Swiss chalet-style building in the centre of a town otherwise notable only for its nearby nuclear power station. Drumming up business didn't turn out to be a problem – but keeping it did. Less than three months later, German police in nearby Waldshut issued a statement relating how a man called 'K. Clemens' had been arrested for the attempted armed robbery of an elderly couple using what turned out to be a toy gun.

Under questioning Mr Clemens broke down in tears, explaining that he was driven to the desperate act in an attempt to make enough money to keep his brothel open. It wasn't that it didn't attract customers, he'd sobbed. It was just that he and the other guys hadn't got the hang of asking for the money upfront. As a result, their lady customers paid what they thought the sex was worth rather than the asking price. Apparently this wasn't enough to keep the brothel open: it was hard not to detect a stifled smirk on the part of the police.

Peter-Georg Biewald, of police media liaison, remembers that Mr Clemens was an attractive young man in a muscle-bound kind of way. Personable, he recalls. A picture he sent me of two of the sex workers, evidently taken for publicity purposes, shows a couple of naked, stocky-looking fellas, one lying on his front, side-on to the camera, all short hair and over-ripe muscle definition, and a back view of the other, who had dark hair and a slightly plump rump that

41

may or may not have had a touch of cellulite. Who could tell in that light?

It's a bad photograph: there is a pole partially obscuring the second man's outline and the red and purple décor of the room looks self-consciously seedy, an impression reinforced by a gas heater in the background, under a varnished pine chalet beam. A woman's touch or an interior decorator wouldn't have gone amiss and the whole scene is reminiscent of the adverts you see at the back of gay men's magazines: think Burt Reynolds meets *Heidi*. It is unusual to see adult men – as opposed to the teenage waifs beloved of the modelling industry – blatantly trying to sell sex to women, and therefore it's probably fair to say that these entre-preneurs were making it up as they went along. If the imagery jars, it may be because they had very few role models to speak of.

So why didn't the business work out? Well, firstly, it did in a way. They clearly attracted enough paying customers through the door to figure out where they were going wrong. One can speculate that had there been a few more days and a few more clients they might have got around to fixing the problem. Perhaps it was a short-lived experiment beaten by time and money?

Another possible construction would be that the women who visited Angels were bargain hunters who sensed a markdown and exploited the pride and foolish optimism of the inexperienced gigolos. Yet even in this cynical scenario, if the clients had thought that the service they'd bought was an experience they wished to repeat, they wouldn't have had any qualms about paying the fee (about £110) asked of them. One can imagine the awkwardness of such a transaction even before adding in a disagreement over the value of the goods: there must have been a very serious problem for the result in many cases to have been breach of contract. Perhaps the token sums left were a symptom of clients' sympathy for an experiment gone wrong? Or guilt money for something that could be justified financially and morally only if the experience were entirely pleasurable – and yet had not been? Whatever feature of the psychosexual landscape these women were navigating by, they evidently felt that they had been overcharged, which was a bit of a shame all round.

The idea of a brothel for women presupposes that there is

something interchangeable about the roles of men and women when it comes to sex: that gender differences can be ignored for the sake of 'a good time' and that nuance disappears in the heat of the moment. But male and female approaches to sex are different.

Using ordinary whorehouses as the template for Angels was surely a mistake, as the gigolos' inability to take the money upfront shows. Perhaps there was some kind of question in the air about whether the ladies would leave happy? And if there were such a doubt, surely this was rather an unprofessional approach for the prostitutes to take, although as it turns out not an unreasonable one? Perhaps these men were under the impression that the service they were selling was contingent upon their own sexual performance rather than the pleasure of their clients, or perhaps the ladies themselves didn't know what it was they were looking for?

And this is the question at the heart of the proposition: what is it that women want? Paying for sex is a choice made by only a minority of people – but as the world's 'oldest profession', prostitution can't be wished away. The issues of coercion, drug abuse and human rights swirl around when the transaction is unfettered by the constraints of law, but Angels was legal and the men who worked there chose to do so. In the same way that some men resort to prostitutes, there will always be some women who have no problem with the idea, whose curiosity gets the better of them or who enjoy the power differential involved in such a deal. There is certainly a market for sexual services for women, but what are its contours?

There are men in every large city who sell themselves like this (usually to other men as well) but brothels for women are practically unheard of. Generally, male prostitutes travel to their clients – the demand isn't perceived as high enough for a business to work the other way around.

It's tempting to ask whether there is something intrinsically different about Swiss and German women that would make them more than usually agreeable to the idea of paying for sex. Yet because Angels shut soon after the attempted mugging, it would be hard to make a case for this. The same question would be universally applicable: namely, if you are a woman and desperate, why pay for sex when you could simply walk into a bar and keep lowering your standards until you find someone who is prepared to sleep with you?

A trip to a brothel is an attempt to fulfil a need that isn't being met elsewhere. Obviously sex is the largest part of it, but sex with another person rather than oneself, and this implies a social need of some kind. Female sex workers often say that many of their clients also want to talk or cry, and while this can sound like a slightly craven attempt to portray themselves as an ambient social service, perhaps that is partly what they are?

So what intimate needs would women pay to have met?

Well, finding out would be a challenge in itself since the fairer sex don't tend to feel oppressed by sexual abstinence in quite the same way that men do, and moreover are very rarely engaged on the subject of what's missing from their lives. The first thing that a successful male gigolo would have to be good at is drawing a client out and listening to her: making her feel that she were the centre of attention. Being in a brothel, where hundreds of other customers have also been would be a bad start, since it would be a reminder from the outset that you were only one of many.

Secondly, the vast majority of women enjoy being pampered and made to feel beautiful. Trips to health spas are eternally popular among those with disposable incomes and this is probably because of the combination of physical pleasure, receiving the undivided attention of a complete stranger who is being paid, and the resulting lack of emotional demands. If one were looking for a template
upon which to base a brothel for women, one could do a lot worse than The Sanctuary in London's Covent Garden, which is a kind of female-only Elysium in an immaculate white space, with fluffy towels.

If The Sanctuary began to offer a wider variety of 'extras' on their tariff, one can speculate that it might go down with customers rather well.

# Europa Island is in both the Indian Ocean and the European Union

L'Ile de Europa has been a French possession since 1897 and is about halfway between the tropical hulk of Madagascar and Mozambique on the African mainland. It's shaped like a cockle or a tadpole with its tail curled round towards its head, the whorl of its fourteen miles of coastline containing only eleven square miles of dense woods and crawling mangrove forests.

It's a wildlife sanctuary for nesting green turtles, birds and reptiles, whose only human inhabitants are a handful of listless French soldiers and meteorologists using Europa as a base from which to survey the Indian Ocean. The sole anchorage is several hundred yards offshore, the runway is unpaved and – if you exclude the depreciation of capital equipment such as radar screens, military boots and, doubtless, the odd snorkel – no economic activity of any kind takes place there.

Yet Europa is 'administered' by the island of Réunion, another French possession on the opposite side of Madagascar. And Réunion is, obscure geographical location notwithstanding, in Europe.

France is unique, having four overseas territories that are 'in' France in every sense apart from their map references. Like Martinique and Guadeloupe in the Caribbean and, most implausibly, French Guiana on the mainland of South America, Réunion is a French *département* – bureaucratically indistinguishable from the *départements* of mainland France.

Réunion is administered by French civil servants who can't believe their luck at getting such a sunny posting. Everything is paid for by the French government, the island is eligible for European funds and – ludicrously, considering the widely-varying ancestry of Réunion's population – the schoolchildren there are taught the same history as all other French children, beginning with: 'Our ancestors, the Gauls …'

France has other overseas territories – Mayotte, Saint-Pierre and Miquelon, French Polynesia, New Caledonia, and Wallis and Fortuna. They are in the analogous position to the fifteen British specks of land scattered over the globe like biscuit crumbs from a high tea finished some time ago: they are French but not in the EU. The four French overseas *départements* differ from these other territories because at some point there was a popular movement on each of them and they were granted closer integration with France.

The existence of these far-flung French territories undermines the argument of any EU politician who doubts Turkey's 'Europeanness' because of its position on the outer edge of 'mainland' Europe. If Réunion is European then the criteria are clearly not geographic but political.

In many senses the EU has always been a work of political architecture designed by the French, who know as much about constructing identities from scratch as anyone else in the world.

You could argue that the French didn't really exist until the end of the 18th century. Before this the term 'France' referred most often to the Ile de France, the *département* in which Paris stands. Half the population of France spoke the Breton, Occitan, Catalan, Basque, Alsatian, Flemish or Provençal languages. It was the postrevolutionary decision to make Paris the bureaucratic hub of a nation that began making French the 'national' language that it is today.

Yet the French state – as opposed to the French nation – existed before the 1789 revolution and this goes to the heart of why the French are so attached to it and its many works. They forgive their state nearly anything because the state effectively created France and the French people, rather than the French people creating the state.

French schoolchildren are taught about former absolutist rulers and their contributions to the formation of the modern French state. François I (1515–47) was a patron of the arts; Henri IV (1589–1610) was a Protestant who renounced his faith to take the crown, setting an example of assimilation that still makes him a hero today; Louis XIV (1643–1715) used the arts to impose his vision of national glory; and Napoleon Bonaparte (1799–1815) built the modern state.

These history lessons emphasise that building anything welldesigned requires leadership. Indeed, persistent authoritarianism and a resulting creativity and flamboyance have marked out the French approach to government over the past few centuries as a force with which to reckon. Most great generals are basically brilliant administrators of large bureaucracies: Napoleon Bonaparte may have died a lonely death on a prison island, but the army of bureaucrats he built to administer the French state marched into the future and still exists today.

This longevity was possible because Napoleon laid his bureaucratic groundwork carefully. The French still pour their best minds into government. They have open competitions for top government jobs, which are intellectual jousting matches that the public can attend. French civil servants receive a job for life and are well paid and well respected. But to receive a promotion in the public sector, even towards the bottom of the food chain, civil servants must study for hours – usually public sector law – and then sit an exam with hundreds of others also hoping to climb to the next level. Most fail at least once.

With all this talent in the public sector, is it any surprise that it was France who built Europe in its own image: a top-down, bureaucratic behemoth with ambition and attitude? They continue to possess the human capital to construct their vision of Europe and, more to the point, they retain a strong belief in the power of government to do good.

French authoritarianism is often mistaken for socialism, especially by Americans with their cautious system of government checks and balances. But the tools of the French state were applied with just as much gusto, perhaps more, by the right-wing General de Gaulle – he enjoyed power politics enough to exclude Britain from the European Community in 1967 largely because he could. Also – although it would probably take a European to point this out – most Americans couldn't reasonably be expected to recognise socialism if it sat on their heads, since they haven't had much experience of it.

The French government believes that it can do anything it sets its collective mind to, and for this it should be – and often is – admired. But France has different priorities to Britain. The French state requires a Muslim girl to set aside her right to wear a headscarf in school for the purpose of assimilation, much as Henri IV set aside his right to be a Protestant because he wished to become King of France. The idea of the 'common good' to which all French should contribute is alive and well in the minds of the French people. This may rankle with civil-rights activists but, when it comes to building a high-speed rail link between Paris and London, no one is in any doubt about which government knows what it's doing.

Europa is a small area of France in the Indian Ocean and it's part of the EU only because France, with its considerable political willpower, wants it to be. The question for the rest of us is: to what extent is the French myth of its own uniqueness – and every country has such a myth – susceptible to an onslaught from other EU member states? France has had its own way for a great many years because it supplied the mindset and the manpower that built the EU.

# The EU constitution is 30 times longer than the US constitution

It's easy to knock the European Union's first stab at a written constitution, which was rejected by the French and Dutch referendums in 2005. It's large, it's unwieldy, and it doesn't look to the naked eye as if it were designed to be read by anyone but lawyers. In comparison with the US constitution, it's a bit of a scary monster.

My copy of the US constitution – including amendments – has seventeen pages, whereas my copy of the European constitution has 487. The US constitution begins: 'We the people ...' The EU version begins: 'His Majesty, the King of the Belgians ...', and God knows the Belgians are always good for a laugh.

But the outward appearance of the document is a result of matching form to function. When the founding fathers of the United States sat down in Philadelphia in 1787 to write their masterpiece of concision, figuratively at least they had a clean sheet of paper. The revolution was over, the British were gone; Jefferson, Madison, Hamilton and the rest were tasked with defining the purpose of their free nation.

However, the EU's constitution was written for a political body that had already existed for about half a century. It represents the consolidation of all the other treaties that have gone before it, negotiated by all its 25 member states. To tear up the previous work done by numberless people over the decades was not an option: the EU demonstrates its purpose in the best way possible – by existing and going about its business.

More than anyone else, the British should be able to appreciate this. Britain makes a virtue out of its own lack of a single US-style document to flap around, citing instead the country's history of adaptation and compromise as a unique gift to the rest of the world. 'We're so cool, we don't need a written constitution', is the general idea as described by British historians and teachers of government. If this attitude sounds a little smug, that's because it often is.

The British government frequently presents itself as remaking

Europe in Britain's image in order to gain popular approval. But in this instance, it has absolutely nothing to offer the EU – at least not anything the EU could usefully emulate – because we don't have our own written constitution.

Britain does have a constitution, of course, but the problem here is mainly linguistic. The word 'constitution' has at least two meanings. It can be both a document and the fundamental principles on which a state is governed – so every state has a constitution of sorts, even if it's only: 'The big man is in charge.'

The lack of a written British constitution presents an intriguing conundrum. The British constitution is simply what happens – at least, this is the nice conceit taught to politics students. It makes them feel that they are getting their money's worth even as the concept evaporates in a puff of smoke.

But if the British constitution simply represents the country's history, it raises the question: what's holding British society together? The US constitution is a statement of fundamental values and beliefs represented by their flag, something they can believe in and respect. It goes to the heart of what the United States of America is. Perhaps in this respect the role of its constitution is unique to the US.

It used to be clear what the glue was in Britain: deference and a resulting civility. Until very recently, British society was one in which everyone knew their place. Class – as defined by one's accent, manners and family – largely defined life chances.

Then a historical anomaly occurred. A generation of grammar school boys and girls achieved political power in the 1960s and for a couple of decades afterwards, before pulling up the ladder behind them by largely destroying the grammar school system. But those two decades were a crucible for social and political change.

Margaret Thatcher was the product of a grammar school education and she set about creatively destroying many of the institutions in which the traditional power of the British constitution lay: the civil service, the unions, the Conservative party. This was her greatest achievement. The days of a small elite believing – with justification – that they were born to rule, appeared to be over.

The style of public life in Britain was changed forever. Deference towards our social superiors has apparently gone, but what has replaced it? What does Britain now know about itself and in what does it believe?

The veneer of deference is gone, but we remain subjects of Her Majesty the Queen and not citizens of our state. We no longer tip our hats to the local bigwigs but read celebrity tittle-tattle in magazines instead, then put them under the cat litter. We struggle to earn more than our neighbours and pay the mortgage, but money doesn't make us happy. We couldn't export our constitutional make-up if we wanted to – or if anybody else wanted it – because it isn't only historically specific, it's in a state of flux and confusion.

The debate about Europe is also in a mess. Britain has a long-standing two-party system, one of which is keen on Europe and the other not, so you would think that it should be easy to produce a balanced public conversation on the subject.

But there is a philosophical problem. The reason why the British Conservatives have appeared anti-European in recent years rests on two main pillars: firstly, a willingness to allow a coalition of xeno-phobes to form around its concerns. And secondly, the unpleasant experience of losing an election, public respect and a sense of purpose after crashing out of the European exchange rate mecha-nism in 1992. The party currently blames Europe for its own failures. Unfortunately, until it works through its resulting identity crisis, the public debate in Britain about Europe will continue to be hopelessly skewed – because the Right has a vested interest in maintaining a level of public confusion. When it purports to be talking about Europe, the Conservative party is often, in fact, talking only about itself.

There are all kinds of quirky and surprising things in the EU constitution. It contains a section about decommissioning the Bohunice nuclear power plant in Slovakia for the same reason that it has sections on the indigenous Sami people of the Arctic and on the national bank of Denmark: these things have passed into European law already. Not including them would have undermined the EU's existing reality. So the document is a historical snapshot rather than a definitive statement.

Also included is a section toward the back called 'The Charter of Fundamental Rights', which is far more like the US constitution than the rest of the EU document. It runs through a series of rights –

including, among others, the right to human dignity, to life, to marry and found a family, to start a business, to live in a high-quality environment, to freedom of expression and the right to education. It's worth a look. Alongside each right, though, the Charter outlines the European case law from which the right was adduced, so even this section wasn't set down on a blank sheet.

Deciding whether to endorse a written European constitution in a referendum, should it ever arise, would involve thinking about what, if anything, the European Union has done for us: whether we are 'better off' for our involvement and not simply in the narrow, economic sense. In order to achieve a meaningful Yes vote, the government would need to get its electorate to focus on the EU and then make a good case in its favour – rather than to allow it to be used it as a cipher for other, ambient political concerns (which is what happened in France and the Netherlands).

Getting an electorate to focus – and then vote – on issues that are wider than those addressed in a national general election would be extremely difficult. There are few precedents either for a government running such a campaign or for an electorate trying to make sense of it. It's likely that such a referendum would turn into a competition of reductive messages, each hoping merely to capture the imagination of the voters. When so little is understood at a popular level about the way the EU works, the field for John-the-Baptist figures, heralding some yet-to-be-revealed truth, would be wide open. EU politics has no shortage of visionaries, either of the utopian or dystopian variety: what would be required is solid information and helpful suggestions.

An unprecedented 60 years of peace in western Europe means that there are generations of people living today who simply wouldn't have existed without this supposedly contentious project. In a referendum on the EU's constitution we would all get an equal say.

# Germans pay tax to the Church unless they declare themselves atheists

A German friend told me that she had recently visited her home country and finally got around to doing something she had put off for ages. 'I opted out of the Church tax', she told me. I blinked. A tax you could choose not to pay didn't sound especially plausible: I had always taken Benjamin Franklin's observation that 'the only things of certainty are death and taxes' as one of my few articles of faith.

No, she explained. Many Germans do it. As a scientist, she had felt for a while that there was some hypocrisy involved in supporting an institution that she believed was based on a big old lie. So she screwed up her courage for an encounter with the powers-that-be, wrote out a few words so she wouldn't get tongue-tied and headed for the local government office.

'I had this big, metaphysical explanation prepared about why I didn't believe in God and when I was ushered into this little room to meet the man with the form, I took a deep breath and launched into it.'

'But it was funny. "Yes, yes. Thank you", he said.' And at this point she imitated the bureaucrat waving his hand at her dismissively. '"Please just sign here."'

Quite aside from the fact that she expected to be hectored, which implies that she has a slightly different relationship with the German state than I do with the British (I expect very little of the British state – least of all for it to take an interest in my personal beliefs), I found this weird on several levels.

Firstly, I had an idea from when I was a politics student that the separation of Church and state was generally considered to be a good thing. Knowing that Germany had a modern constitution pressed on it by the Allies after the Second World War, I was surprised that the German government is allowed to collect money on behalf of the Church.

Also – and this is pure culture clash for me – it's considered normal in Germany to pay this tax even though you can choose not to. By birth, my friend was involved in a spiritual organisation so embedded in everyday life that the state taxed her for it: a clue that the Germans have a very different approach to religion.

Nearly two-thirds of Germans – 55 million people – pay the Church tax, or *Kirchensteuer*, which piles up as billions of euros every year. According to the most recent figures available, 26.6 million of these people are Roman Catholic and 26.3 million are Protestant. Money also goes to synagogues, for obvious historical reasons, and to Greek and Russian Orthodox Churches and Seventh Day Adventists. All these denominations are established as 'corporations in public law'. The idea is that by making the relationship purely financial (the government keeps the cost of collecting the tax), they avoid concerns about having the most powerful institutions in the country working for each other. The amount of money each faith group receives is directly proportional to the number of Germans who are members of their denomination and pay the tax.

'It is amazing how few Germans opt out really, isn't it?' said Dr Christopher Clarke, a specialist in German history at Cambridge University. 'Many of them have ceased to be Christian in a faith sense, but a lot of functions in German society are still seen as intrinsically Christian. It is seen as natural that the Church should be involved in caring for the elderly and for some schools, for instance – and that is the justification for continuing to pay the tax. It's a bit like being a member of Amnesty International.'

The money is spent on salaries, building maintenance and good works in the community. There are Church-run hospitals, nursing homes and day-care centres, as well as Church-sponsored humanitarian aid and assistance programmes in the developing world.

The German government chooses which religious organisations are suitable to be a 'corporation in law' and, since there are more than 600 different faith-based organisations with tax-free status, the issue of which of them is entitled to claim their share of the tithe is a matter of public debate. There's nothing to prevent Germans from opting out of the tax and donating 9 per cent of their income tax to the religious organisation of their choice, but the state's recognition gives organisations additional legitimacy.

Although freedom to worship is guaranteed in Germany's Basic Law, religious organisations don't gain the state's acceptance as a matter of course. Scientology, for example, applied for tax exemption and the German judicial system ruled against it, arguing that it was a 'commercial enterprise with a history of taking advantage of vulnerable individuals and an extreme dislike of any criticism'. The judgement also stated the government's concern that 'the organisation's totalitarian structure and methods may pose a risk to Germany's democratic society'. Ouch.

Even more ticklish is the case of the Jehovah's Witnesses, who were persecuted by the Nazis. Around 5,000 are estimated to have died in concentration camps because they refused to renounce their religious beliefs. Jehovah's Witnesses wouldn't recognise allegiance to an earthly government, thinking of themselves solely as part of the Kingdom of Jehovah. They refused to raise their arms in Nazi salutes on principle.

But in modern Germany, the concern about Jehovah's Witnesses relates to their medical doctrines. Although there's sympathy for any group that resisted Nazism so comprehensively, society has difficulty accepting a religion that forbids blood transfusions for children – who have probably not chosen their faith – as well as for adults. Largely for this reason, Jehovah's Witnesses are not allowed to participate in the Church tax.

The United States was the first country to effectively separate Church from state, through the first amendment to the US constitution, and it was done as much to protect the wrangling sects of its Puritan citizens from the state as the other way around. The Quakers, Shakers and myriad other Protestant splinter groups had voyaged all the way to the New World in order to achieve the freedom to worship – and they were not going to allow any pesky government to interfere with that hard-won right. Yet to this day, it's inconceivable that a US president could get elected without professing a belief in God.

For similar historic reasons, the French are also extremely hot on separation. The post-revolutionary association of the Catholic Church with the overthrown aristocratic government was strong enough to guarantee that, more than two centuries later, debate rages when a Muslim girl wishes to wear a headscarf in a state-run school. Islam isn't currently involved in Germany's Church tax either.

The phrase 'separation of Church and state' implies that the two can be either separate or not, but doesn't really do justice to the full spectrum of possible relationships. For instance, although Britain is one of the most godless nations in the world, its Queen is both Head of State and Defender of the Faith. This is an accretion of influence that, were it not so meaningless to so many Britons in practice, could be seen as profoundly dangerous. Imagine the kind of power that she could wield if either of her roles were perceived as anything more than decorative. You could be looking at a kind of religious totalitarianism in which we could all be forced to go to the races, toting matching shoes and handbags.

By contrast, Germany has a major political party called the Christian Democrats, whose existence represents many people's resistance to the process of secularisation. It uses the term *Schöpfungsordnung*, which means 'the order of creation', to justify many of its positions, including those on abortion and the environment. It suggests a need to be humanist but with a respect for the world as God's creation, which includes ponds, trees and climate as much as people. German spirituality is out and proud.

# Spain would rather Gibraltar were bankrupt than British

Cheap petrol appears to be the only thing that the Spanish really like about Gibraltar. There's a garage just inside the border of the tiny three-mile-square British territory that sells more petrol than any other on the Iberian Peninsula. And why? Gibraltar has a lower tax regime than Spain and the Spanish like to pop over and make the most of it.

It's hard to blame them. But then you also can't blame them for being angry about Gibraltar itself. It's an affront to their dignity. Britain captured Gibraltar during the War of Spanish Succession in 1704; Spain finally ceded it to Britain at the end of this war in the Treaty of Utrecht of 1713. Diplomatically its British credentials are unimpeachable, even if its only borders are with Spain and the deep blue sea.

Gibraltar's location makes it a gatehouse to the Mediterranean, one that is no less useful now than it was during the Napoleonic wars. Ships still need to refuel and get fresh provisions before heading in to or out of the Atlantic. There are also illegal migration from North Africa and terrorism to consider these days, but strategically Gibraltar is exactly what it has always been – very useful.

The reasons why the Spanish are annoyed have changed, though. Initially, the British military prevented Spain from reclaiming Gibraltar. It was a Royal Naval port and eventually a military airfield too, bristling with squaddies. Spain was outgunned …

But now it's simply outvoted. Gibraltar's last referendum on the subject in 2002 resulted in a ratio of 99 to 1 against the idea of joint Spanish and British sovereignty – so Gibraltar remains British.

In the 300 years since the Treaty of Utrecht, the isthmus has developed its own identity and acquired a population that isn't very Spanish at all. Most of the people who live there speak a Spanish dialect, but the everyday language is English and the town is like a sunnier version of Portsmouth on the south coast of England. The residents are the offspring of British soldiers and sailors, with a good sprinkling of Sephardic Jews from North Africa and others.

Its peculiar smallness has called for a bit of creativity in how it makes a living. Since 1967, when the reality of a closed border with Spain (thanks to General Franco) began to bite, Gibraltar has become an international tax centre. It offers banking and other financial services for wealthy people all over the world, who would pay more tax if they banked at home. This now makes up around 35 per cent of its Gross Domestic Product, and also makes it one of the few places in Europe where it isn't unusual to see an advertisement on the back of a newspaper asking for experienced futures traders.

Gibraltar joined the EU in 1973 at the same time as Britain – it's the only international tax centre which is also a member – and has a unique status: its constituency is folded in with the West Country on mainland Britain. 'Franco had shut the frontier', explained Peter Montegriffo, a lawyer and former Gibraltarian foreign minister. 'It was felt that the framework of the EU would one day help establish normality with Spain. And at the time it had no impact on our tax regime.'

'But then in the early nineties there was a movement towards tax harmonisation within the EU and Gibraltar began to be caught up in the general tide.'

Tax harmonisation in the EU is a work in progress. Gibraltar is currently appealing against a rule that Gibraltar's tax regime should be the same as the UK's. If the rule stands, Gibraltar's economy will have to be completely remade.

There was a point in 2002 when it looked as if the EU's competition commission might backdate the tax owed by businesses based in Gibraltar. This would have bankrupted the place and sent Gibraltar into political turmoil. According to a report in *The Business* newspaper in September 2004, Spain was the only EU member apart from Britain and Gibraltar that contributed to the EU investigation. A dose of political turmoil is also, realistically, the only situation in which Spain stands any chance of getting Gibraltar back.

'Its main motivation is political: it wants to undermine Gibraltar because it is a part of a campaign to soften us up. But tax harmonisation is something that is happening across Europe. There is also an enormous difference between northern and southern European culture on these matters,' said Mr Montegriffo.

'When Spain looks at Gibraltar it doesn't understand what is meant by "international tax centre". It just sees something disreputable. Part of the problem we face is a gulf of comprehension. In their eyes, what we do is illegitimate.'

'For a Spaniard there is no distinction between tax evasion and tax avoidance, whereas to the Americans or English, one is illegal and the other is a way of getting large amounts of capital in one place.'

'The Spanish conflate our tax status with other parts of Gibraltar's behaviour in the past – the tobacco smuggling, for instance. In the eyes of Madrid, Gibraltar is one big pirates' den. They point out that there are 50,000 companies in Gibraltar and only 30,000 residents, and cite this as if it were evidence of illicit activities. But from our point of view it is a bit like saying that there are so many hotel beds in the Costa del Sol and only so many residents.'

Spain's history of aggression against Gibraltar has included creating frontier delays, refusing to recognise Gibraltarian phone prefixes on Spanish exchanges, and forcing cruise liners to choose between the two places for mooring.

Michael Llamas, Gibraltar's legal advisor in Brussels, says that Spain's behaviour is one of the main reasons why the vote against shared British and Spanish sovereignty is always so overwhelming.

'Perhaps if their tactics were based on seduction rather than aggression they would have more success – a growing number of Gibraltarians are buying second homes in Spain and there is a great deal of social intercourse.'

'In an ideal world, the European Commission could be a part of the solution to the problem. Whether we like it or not, Europe is a place where sovereignty is being dissolved. The solution could be one where no one wins and everyone wins because sovereignty has simply become a different thing', he said.

The accession of ten new EU countries in 2004 brought the issue of tax to the fore, because one of the best hopes that several of these countries have for attracting inward investment is their lower tax regimes. Estonia, for instance, actually offers a rate of zero per cent to companies under some circumstances.

If the drive towards tax harmonisation continues, Gibraltar isn't the only place in the EU that would be in trouble. But it is the only one that would face bankruptcy over a 300-year-old dispute.

# Without Islam, Europe wouldn't exist

Boabdil, Spain's last Moorish ruler, sat astride his horse on the most distant hilltop from which he could still see the soaring pinnacles of his lost palace, the Alhambra. It was the 15th century, he had been beaten militarily by Queen Isabella and he was leaving his land, knowing it was the last time he would ever lay eyes on his birthright. Tears rolled down his face and he felt the pull of the 800 years during which his forefathers had ruled the plains and mountains of Andalucía. He experienced the centuries at that moment as if they were a vast empty space into which his heart was falling.

This high, lonely vantage point is known as The Moor's Last Sigh. Boabdil's name is a Western corruption of Abu Abdullah, but he was also known as *ci zogoybi* – 'the unlucky', or *el chico* – 'the little'. He must have felt very small that day.

Because legend has it that, as he sat there in tears with his horse lurching beneath him, his mother, who had survived the recent siege of the Alhambra alongside him, finally lost patience with the son whom she had always felt didn't match up to his father. 'Weep!' she cried. 'Weep like a woman for that which you could not keep as a man!'

If this were a film, at this point it would turn into a Monty Python. Terry Jones would be revealed as the unlikely mother, and powerful North African music would cut abruptly. 'Thanks, Mum', the unlucky son would reply, wondering why he had brought the old bag with him after all. 'Just what I need at a time like this – a bit of moral support.'

Classical Islam ruled Spain for 800 years. It wasn't camping out. It was the best thing in Europe for the better part of a millennium. During the time known as Europe's Dark Ages, Islam was a beacon of public libraries, poetry, liberal humanism, classical scholarship, engineering, medicine and other science. Islam invented the university. In many ways Europe is a product of Islam.

And Europe is an idea as well as a geographical location. It was exported as a concept with its own colonials to Australia, the

Americas and anywhere else they went, so that the things we most readily associate with the word are bigger than the place itself.

Similarly, many of those same ideas were originally imported to Europe from elsewhere, though at the time few people were inclined to give much credit to the Muslims, or the 'Saracen', because then how could you send your soldiers on a crusade against them?

It has long been accepted in academic literature that the Renaissance was partly a result of a flood of classical Greek manuscripts and scholars arriving in Italy after political upheavals in Constantinople. Without these manuscripts and, crucially, the ability to translate them (done largely via Arabic), the Renaissance could never have been what it was: a confabulation of money and ideas which allowed western Europe to invent its own largely mythical history involving direct lineage from the Greeks and the Roman Empire. Without the Renaissance there would have been no Enlightenment – and then, before you can say the *Rubaiyat of Omar Khayyam*, Europe as we know and imagine it today would not exist at all.

There is also the question of how one forms an identity in the first place. Although it is normal to speak of one's genes, one's family upbringing and surroundings, is it not also the case that people often form their identity in opposition to someone else? Many European countries have mythologies about their national Christian identity as a result of battles – real or imaginary – against Islam.

Spain has Pelayo, who inflicted the first defeat on the peninsula's Moorish rulers in 718, beginning the Reconquista – reconquering – that took seven more centuries. France's first epic story was *La Chanson de Roland*, about a battle between a French knight and an Islamic invader in the Pyrenees. The Germans too have a national story of Teutonic knights going east to Jerusalem and returning home to apply the spirit of the crusades against the Poles, the Finns, the Balts and the Lithuanians. One of the defining images of Hitler was of him wearing a suit of armour and facing towards the East.

'Europe as we know it would be inconceivable without Islam', said Tim Winter, of Cambridge University's Faculty of Divinity. 'No one would seriously contest that. The design for English cathedrals reflects the skills that were brought back by the stonemasons and engineers at the time of the crusades. The Gothic style, many of the engineering techniques, the stained glass windows – these are Islamic and not indigenous to the European nations.'

'The presence of types of weaving, textiles, carpets, the introduction of paper, the introduction of dedicated hospitals, the virtual monopoly of Arabic texts at medical schools in Europe until the 16th century, the prevalence of the teaching of Aristotle, all meant that Europe was fundamentally reorientated by the neighbouring, far more successful civilisation of Islam.'

The relative lack of Greek manuscripts until their arrival from Constantinople, and the dominance of Rome and the Catholic Church, meant that previously many scholars had not seen the point of knowing more than one classical language: Latin. A flood of new ideas poured forth once the many works written in Greek were translated into Latin via Arabic.

'So, for instance, Thomas Aquinas – a key figure in the development of Western philosophy – refers to two figures more than any others', said Dr Winter.

'He refers to "The Philosopher", by whom he means Aristotle, and he refers to "The Commentator", by whom he means Ibn Rushd, who wrote the commentaries for many of Aristotle's key works. So medieval Christendom was very different after the Arab and Islamic influence.'

In addition to this intellectual underpinning of our societies, Dr Winter pointed out that there is also practical evidence of Islam's influence right under our noses.

'The quintessential irascible English squire gets up in the morning and has a coffee, which originated in a Turkish bazaar. He has a croissant, which was baked first by Viennese pastry cooks to celebrate their defeat of the Ottomans in 1687. His feet are likely to rest on a carpet which is Turkish or Persian.'

'He is likely to have horses which, if they are thoroughbred, come from those brought over in the 18th century from Arabia. If he goes to the pub, it might be called the Saracen's Head or some other recollection of traditional English engagement with the Arabic world. If he goes to church he is worshipping in a structure which would probably still be Romanesque but for the enormous transformation that Islamic style brought to British sacred architecture.'

'So his classic stick-in-the-mud xenophobia can be readily blown apart if only he can be brought to realise that many of these symbols are of Islamic origin. But he is unlikely to want to look that in the eye unless it is brought to his attention.'

And then there is the obvious: the word Europe. According to Homer, Europa was a maiden desired by the Greek god Zeus, who took the form of a white bull. He carried her away over the sea to Crete, where she bore him three sons, including King Minos. According to the story, this extraordinary beauty, Europa, was dark-eyed and her father was called Agenor, or Phoenix, the King of Phoenicia. And where was Phoenicia?

In the Middle East.

# The paint on Berlin's Holocaust memorial was produced by the same company that manufactured Zyklon B

Zyklon B was the chemical that the Nazis used to murder millions in their gas chambers. Its generic name was prussic acid and it was originally used as an insecticide. Degesch didn't invent it, but the company did have a monopoly on its production. The innovation that Degesch made – and very lucrative it turned out to be – was demonstrating that it could also be used on human beings.

When mass exterminations in the gas chambers of Auschwitz-Birkenau began, the German authorities asked the company if it could make a version that didn't have Zyklon B's characteristic smell – something that wouldn't alert their victims to its presence before they were killed. Degesch was worried: the company directors made it clear that they were concerned about the business implications.

They complained that their patent, on which their monopoly was based, was for Zyklon B with the characteristic smell. Without it, alarmingly, they would be open to competition from other companies, and their profits would diminish. Nevertheless Nazi heads were put together, Degesch was pacified with promises, and the odourless gas pellets were manufactured.

One-and-a-half million people are believed to have been murdered at Auschwitz using Zyklon B.

Degesch was owned 42.5 per cent by a company called Deutsche Gold und Silberschneidenanstalt, now known as Degussa. It was Degussa that manufactured the anti-vandal paint to prevent neo-Nazis defacing the Holocaust memorial in Berlin. There was an outcry about the connection, but it passed.

A company called IG Farben owned another 42.5 per cent of Degesch, and also owned a third of Degussa. IG Farben was no minor league player and has been held up as the single most crucial manufacturing element of Hitler's war effort. Its production of synthetic oil and rubber freed German diplomacy from the shackles of its enemies' oil wells and rubber groves. Albert Speer, the Reich minister for armaments, decided that Germany couldn't win the war only on 12 May 1944, when nearly 1,000 bombers from the US 8th Air Force reduced IG Farben's biggest synthetic oil plant at Leuna to rubble.

Executives on the board of IG Farben were called to account at the Nuremburg trials: not only for manufacturing Zyklon B, but also for other crimes. For instance, when the Third Reich invaded other European countries, IG Farben was on hand to strip their former foreign competitors of any useful technological innovations or materials.

But perhaps most shockingly, IG Farben built a manufacturing plant at Auschwitz to capitalise on slave labour made available to them by the Nazis. So vast was this installation that it used as much electricity in a day as the whole of Berlin. 25,000 of Auschwitz's doomed slaves are estimated to have died building it.

Slave labour is something that accountants have lost the knack of integrating into their calculations these days. But try to imagine not paying one's workforce – and the manner of profit you could extract from an already successful product once the element of human resources vanished from the accounting books.

Money for forced labour changed hands from IG Farben's accounts to the Waffen SS as a token thank-you for the SS's co-operation and for their guards – no good, after all, paying for slaves if they can escape. It was three Reichsmarks a day for an unskilled labourer and one-and-a-half for a child.

But there was another important consideration for IG Farben and the SS: both parties realised that concentration camp inmates couldn't be as productive as free, well-fed German workers, so their usefulness was calculated at 75 per cent efficiency.

The average weight loss to an individual at IG Farben's Auschwitz factory – known as Monowitz – was between six-and-a-half and nine pounds a week. After three weeks in the place they were unrecognisable even to their families, and after three months they were either dead or so unfit for work that they were sent to nearby Birkenau for extermination. Each detachment of between 400 and

500 people returned to their bunks in the evening carrying the corpses of between five and twenty fellow inmates, so the guards could account for everyone.

As Joseph Borkin wrote in his book *The Crime and Punishment of IG Farben*:

> The construction of IG Auschwitz has assured IG a unique place in business history. By adopting the theory and practice of Nazi morality, it was able to depart from the conventional economics of slavery, in which slaves are traditionally treated as capital equipment to be maintained and serviced for optimum use and depreciated over a normal lifespan.
>
> Instead, IG reduced slave labour to a consumable raw material, a human ore from which the mineral of life was systematically extracted. When no usable energy remained, the living dross was shipped to the gassing chambers and cremation furnaces of the extermination centre at Birkenau, where the SS recycled it into the German war economy – gold teeth for the Reichsbank, hair for mattresses and fat for soap. Even the moans of the doomed became a work incentive, exhorting the remaining inmates to greater effort.

When the war was over, 24 IG Farben executives were indicted at Nuremburg. Twelve were convicted of either slavery and mass murder, or plunder and spoliation. The maximum sentence, received by two of them, was eight years in prison and the lightest was only one-and-a-half years. The prosecution staff were outraged. The chief prosecutor, an American called Josiah DuBors, wrote a book about it called *The Devil's Chemists*, describing the sentences as 'light enough to please a chicken thief'. People receive harsher penalties today for one murder. So ask yourself: could it ever be possible to atone for the deaths of 1.5 million people?

According to one BBC report, more than 6,000 German companies have contributed to a fund that the German government set up in 2000 to provide a £3.5 billion settlement for an estimated 200,000 to 300,000 former slave labourers. The majority of these survivors live in Eastern Europe, although obviously there are fewer left alive with every passing year. This was one of many similar initiatives set up by industrialists hoping to help expunge the stain of their historical involvement with the Nazis.

Heavy industry, banks, clothing, food and household goods manufacturers: you name the sector and there were well-known companies, household names, involved. Indeed, how could they not be? To build a multinational usually takes several generations, and for most European industry, just surviving the Second World War involved an element of co-operation with the Nazis. If their businesses had failed because they disapproved of what this involved, we wouldn't now know their names.

Many of the most successful European businesses carry their shame buried deep in company reports, where the amount they are contributing to reparation funds is often described as 'a good-will gesture'. Their goodwill, however, has frequently been brought on by the threat of indictment – damaging both financially and politically – from survivors of the Nazis' victims, most often in the US. Many non-European companies are in the same position: even that most American of enterprises, Ford, had a plant in Cologne where slave labour was used.

Bayer, DaimlerChrysler, Volkswagen, Deutsche Bank, Krupp, Zurich Insurance, the Credit Suisse Group are all in this position. The chemical giant BASF was one of the companies created when IG Farben was dismantled in 1951.

Companies are constantly being taken over, broken down and having shares bought by other outfits. Like water in a vast ocean, international capital has a fluid quality that often makes it impossible to truly separate any giant of industry from another, although, as with molecules of water, it could be done by those with the time and the inclination.

When the row about the anti-vandal paint blew up, Wolfgang Thierse, the speaker of Germany's lower house of parliament, said: 'Many other German firms which were in some way linked to Nazi crimes determine our economic life and are involved in projects that remember the Nazi time. It's a question of where we draw the line.'

Would it ever be possible to wash this money clean?

# There is a Bosnian war criminal in the Swedish prison system, which is renowned for its horse-riding, swimming lessons and dance classes

Sweden has a reputation for liberalism that extends as far as its prison service. It jails a tiny proportion of its population (68 per 100,000) in comparison with Britain (139), Portugal (131) and Spain (126) – the three west European nations with the largest number of incarcerated adults. However, Latvia has the largest proportion of any European nation (361), closely followed by Estonia (337) and Lithuania (303). And these are thrown into relief by Russia's 638 per 100,000 of the population and the US's 686, which is the highest proportion in the world.

'When they leave, they should be at least as good as when they came in,' said Lars Nylen, the head of Sweden's prison service, who habitually refers to prisoners as 'clients'. 'The object is to make them better.'

As with all prison populations, Sweden's jails contain a large proportion of educational under-achievers and drug addicts, though a surprisingly large number of the convicted – around 30 per cent – have actually been found guilty of drink-driving. Education and the removal of drug dependency are the most important tasks set for prisoners in a culture that places a very high value on work.

Lutheranism suggests that most problems can be solved through work. In Scandinavia's remarkably homogenous communities, this belief has transcended its religious origins to become an organising principle for everyday life.

So, unsurprisingly, an emphasis on work is also central to the Swedish prison system. When not taking part in programmes – which can include horse-riding, dance classes and swimming, as well as cooking one's own food – the average inmate spends his or her days in factories and workshops, toiling for rehabilitation. 'But the one who is hardest to rehabilitate is the one with a diagnosis as a psychopath,' said Mr Nylen.

Biljana Plavsic could have been invented to test the purpose of a Swedish prison. A former president of Bosnia-Herzegovina, she pleaded guilty to crimes against humanity at a tribunal in The Hague in February 2003. She was sentenced to eleven years and, as the United Nations' war crimes tribunal has no prison of its own, sent to serve her time at Hinseberg prison, 125 miles from Stockholm.

Current estimates are that 100,000 people were murdered during the Bosnian inter-ethnic conflict that Plavsic instigated and encouraged, although the real number will never be known. She was regarded as a hard-liner even by Slobodan Milosevic, whose own actions during the 1990s represent a catalogue of blasted flesh.

A biologist, former Fulbright scholar and Dean of the faculty of Natural Sciences and Mathematics at the University of Sarajevo, Biljana Plavsic has gone on record describing Muslims as 'genetically deformed', adding at another time: 'We are disturbed by the fact that the number of marriages between Serbs and Muslims has increased … because mixed marriages lead to an exchange of genes between ethnic groups and thus to a degeneration of Serb nationhood.' At the time of writing she is the most senior figure to have been convicted of Bosnian war crimes.

To talk to Graham Hand, Britain's ambassador to Sarajevo from 1998 to 2001, is to get a strong sense of the moral relativism involved in picking one's way through the former Yugoslavia in the late 1990s.

'Biljana Plavsic was found guilty of crimes against humanity, so there's nothing to add in that respect,' he said from his office in St James's, London, where he now organises British consultancies around the world.

'I knew her in the late 1990s, as the elected head of a Serbian sub-state. She was a dignified woman with considerable presence. I didn't ask her what had gone on when she was President in the early 1990s, but had I done so her attitude would almost certainly have been that the past was over and we should move on.'

His response to the memory of the Serbs' 'Iron Lady', was warm, empathetic and reminiscent of the way in which many British men speak about Margaret Thatcher in her glory days – there was respect, admiration and not a little awe for a woman who knew how to wield power.

'For a long time she believed that she would get away with it,' he explained. 'She was popular with Western governments for several years after the worst of the killing because she was playing our game. She talked a rational kind of language at a time and in a place where most people were shifty, craven and full of bullshit ... When she said something – and she said some pretty hard things – you at least knew that she meant it. She got a lot of sympathy from the Americans.'

'Eventually she became aware that the UN prosecutors were on her case and that they would not be deflected by comments like "there's been a misunderstanding". She must have known that there would either be a reckoning or she could go into hiding.'

'But she is much too dignified a person to have chosen to hide as Mladic and Karadzic have done. I was nearly sent to Banja Luka to bring her in, you know ... To be honest, it's not a job I would have welcomed anyway ... there was a dignity about her. Whether she preserves that in her Swedish prison, I don't know.'

Plavsic was 72 years old when she was convicted of crimes against humanity. At the time, she said that she didn't believe there would be anything to gain by seeking a reduced sentence, since even a moderate ten-year term would, in all likelihood, mean spending the rest of her life behind bars.

And what is that life? Hinseberg jail incorporates an old castle and, as described by its manager, Karl Anders Lonnberg, it has 'a garden with plenty of old trees. It's a beautiful place – not like a normal prison.' Because she is past the Swedish retirement age, Plavsic doesn't have to work, the single concept upon which the system, with its explicit goal of rehabilitation, is built. This means that she is effectively outside of the jail's ideological aims and constraints.

In short, to attempt to rehabilitate someone so elderly, so eminent in her various fields, and so far beyond the Swedish prison system's usual realm of teaching drug-addled youngsters to read and write, would be to hope for the impossible.

She spends her time writing and has produced a memoir called *I Testify* from her prison cell – it received a tiny print run and hasn't been translated from Serbo-Croat. She also wrote a letter to a Serbian newspaper, *Politika*, in 2003, accusing the prison authorities of pumping foul air into her cell during the night. The claim brings to mind the saying from Euripides that 'those whom the gods wish to destroy, first they make mad' – this could bring a scrap of comfort to those interested in a more Old Testament approach to war criminals.

Otherwise it would be hard to disagree with Mr Hand's assessment of the situation, on hearing about her rambling prison with its gardens. 'If I had to guess, I would say that she would be content with that, because she has come from this dreadful time in the Balkans. She has ended up in a fully democratic country with everything she needs and not much more', he mused. 'I would guess she is not unhappy.'

# The twelve stars on the EU flag are a symbol of the Virgin Mary

In January 1995, as a young reporter doing some work experience at the *Irish Times*, I was given a job to do. Sweden, Austria and Finland had joined the EU, increasing the number of member states from twelve to fifteen. The news editor wanted to know whether the number of stars on the flag would also increase.

So I got on the phone to the European Commission in Dublin and put it to them. The answer was no – the flag would remain the same – and the reason for this was more complicated than I expected.

It turned out that the twelve stars design had originally belonged to the Council of Europe, which is an entirely separate organisation to the EU. It came up with the flag in 1955. The Council had fourteen members, but 'twelve', according to the voice on the other end of the phone, is a 'symbol of perfection'.

'The number has always had a superstitious significance. Some people think that there is a link to Mariolatry – devotion to the Virgin Mary. Traditionally it has been common to represent the Virgin with twelve stars around her brow', said the Commission's spokesman.

There was no denying it. A small amount of research produced the conclusion that twelve stars around Mary's head is known as a 'stellarium' in Renaissance iconography and is a way of showing her as the Virgin of the Immaculate Conception. In medieval scholarship, this incarnation of Jesus's mother is closely linked to a passage in Revelation 12:1, which talks about 'a woman clothed with the sun, with the moon under her feet and a crown of twelve stars on her head'.

In 1984, the European Community – which became the European Union in 1992 – adopted the Council of Europe's flag, along with Beethoven's Ode to Joy, as part of a rebranding exercise.

The Community did have twelve members at the time. Because of this and probably also because the number of stars on the American flag coincides with the number of states in the union, many people assume that there is a similar link for the stars on the EU flag. In fact it was simply a coincidence.

The story that the twelve stars would stay went on page two of the *Irish Times* and everyone at the paper was happy – especially because the BBC, for a few aberrant days, illustrated their stories about EU enlargement with an EU flag displaying fifteen stars. So much for the competition.

But in the intervening years, while there are still twelve stars on the EU flag, other things have changed. Turkey is now a serious contender for EU membership, and Bosnia and Albania, both predominantly Muslim countries, also want to join. In this light, a piece of Catholic iconography at the heart of the EU suddenly seems an unfortunate choice.

By today's standards of political correctness, it is insensitive to use a symbol of the Virgin Mary to represent a continent that contains large swathes of Protestant population, and a number of other religions. Could it really have been intentional?

Conspiracy theorists on the internet, among them the Reverend Sir Ian Paisley, see the European Union as a vast Papist plot and have seized upon the symbolism of the flag as proof. There are also rumours on Catholic websites that Arsene Heitz, the artist who designed the flag, came up with the idea while walking in the Rue de Bac in Paris, where the Virgin Mary is sometimes said to appear to the devout.

What is definitely known, though, is that Count Coudenhove-Kalergi, who led the Council of Europe's flag committee in 1955, was a devout and learned Catholic – he at first proposed the emblem of a cross for the flag. Unsurprisingly, this was vetoed by Turkey.

Then, stars on a blue background were mooted but there was a disagreement about how many there should be. There were fourteen members of the Council of Europe … but twelve stars were arrived at. It was a good number, a lucky number and a symbol of perfection. Plus it would have pleased any Catholics on the committee who were aware of the symbolism and had wanted a cross in the first place.

In 1956, the Council of Europe gave Strasbourg Cathedral a stained glass window of the Virgin Mary wearing a crown of twelve stars, by the artist Max Ingrand. And in 1993, the European Union's official Christmas card showed a floating female figure carrying a crown of twelve stars. It was a detail from the ceiling of the Palazzo Barberini in Rome, and the figure is about to place the crown on the head of the Woman of the Apocalypse from the Book of Revelation.

So does it matter about the flag? Turkey's application to join the EU will be fraught with disagreements about what the purpose of the EU is. The French in particular have a problem with the application, which could end Turkey's European dream, since it has to be accepted by all existing members of the EU. If it did join in 2015, current projections suggest that it would be more populous than Germany, making it the union's largest nation, as well as its poorest.

Having an Islamic country inside the European Union would reposition Europe as a big player in the Middle East, enhancing its ability to act elsewhere. But in attempting to make this happen, there would be many obstacles to overcome, one of which could be the apparently careless symbolism of the EU flag.

Twelve stars are a powerful totem for Europe's Christian culture and history. The question is, how much does it matter to Europe's future?

# The Russian Space Agency agreed to allow a porn film to be shot on Mir

*Weightlessness will bring new forms of erotica. About time too.*
Arthur C. Clarke

In November 1997, a Muscovite director called Yuri Kara announced that he hoped to send two actors into space to shoot a film that would include an explicit sex scene. He had raised £13 million, he said, and wished to make a movie based on a novel called *The Mark of Cassandra* by the Russian author Chingiz Aitmatov. It's about a renegade cosmonaut who refuses to leave a space station slated for abandonment, declaring that he will orbit the Earth for the rest of his days. Ground control sends a woman to seduce him and lure him home.

There was much excitement and names were bandied about. Three Russian actors (Vladimir Steklov, Natalia Gromnshkina and Olga Kabo) passed preliminary medical tests allowing them to train as astronauts at Russia's Star City, Gary Oldman and Sean Penn were mentioned in connection with the project and a Hollywood producer was brought on board. Yuri Koptev, the General Director of the Russian Space Agency (RSA), was quoted as saying: 'This is an exotic project but the RSA considers it possible in order to get additional money. Life has made us change our mentality and one has to overcome snobbery when dozens of millions of dollars are involved.'

Meanwhile Kara stoked the flames by releasing to the press tantalising pictures of the lovely Natalia Gromnshkina, who was 'fresh from drama school'. He told the breathless public that, after raising the money, the most difficult part of the project would be getting the actors out of their spacesuits for weightless sex.

Kara drafted in John Daly, a British movie producer based in Hollywood (and who produced *The Terminator*) to be his bridge to the American market. 'They had the backing of a Russian oil company,' Daly recalled. 'And it was represented by a politician in the Duma. I was approached by this consortium, which wanted me to produce and co-write the script and I was very interested.'

'I met Yuri Kara once and he told me that the plan was to try and shoot on Mir, although when you think of the technical difficulties involved, the whole thing seems quite mad now. I suppose we could have trained an astronaut to use a camera, shot for a few days on Mir, then built a replica set on Earth.'

'In fact I visited Steklov when he was doing basic training. He completed the course – so I guess you could say that there is a spare astronaut loose out there, disguised as an actor. But the fact of the matter is that the Russian Space Agency didn't get the money that they had been promised. They trained this guy up, which must have cost thousands, if not millions, the backers didn't come up with the money and then Mir came tumbling down. It was always a race against time.'

The end of Mir was a symbolic moment for the Russians, whose transformation during the lifetime of the space station from superpower to gangster economy had already been a humbling experience. After fifteen years, Mir crashed into the South Pacific, as intended, on 23 March 2003. It had circled the Earth 88,000 times, travelled 2.2 billion miles and had been man's first home in space. Most scientists agree that the science done on the station was negligible. But its achievement was nonetheless awesome: Mir made space-flight routine.

By the end of its life, hundreds of astronauts (or cosmonauts as the Russians have always called them) had lived on the station, which looked like a gigantic television aerial hurtling through our luminous, blue-black near space. These men and women were largely anonymous – who knows the names of modern astronauts? – and the day-to-day routine on Mir was, by the sound of it, quite dull. 'Looking at the stars, pissing in jars' is the prosaic description of life above the Earth by those who have been there and done it. But in terms of the physiological and psychological demands placed on humans in space, the Russians on Mir put in the spade-work that space programmes will be drawing on for decades.

By the time the film was mooted, the Russian space programme was in financial trouble, along with just about everything else associated with the Russian government. *The Mark of Cassandra* was one of many increasingly wild money-making projects that were discussed with the aim of keeping Mir aloft – other ideas included an American TV game show with trips to the space station as prizes, and space tourism, which did actually take place for a handful of multimillionaires.

When Mir came down, there was an outpouring of grief on the streets of Moscow for the loss of one of the most powerful symbols of the former Soviet Empire's might. For a country to even have a space programme suggests that politicians have been able to fight and win (or avoid) a debate about whether the research is valuable relative to a country's more pressing needs – the education, health-care and other requirements that are all paid for from the same pot. It indicates wealth, power and prestige: it is the cathedral of science projects, for which motivation is as important as practical need.

*The Mark of Cassandra* was discussed as soft porn and, in one sense, what better reminder could there be that space technology would be pointless if it were not for the people behind it and their all-too-human impulses: political, financial, emotional and sexual. Wherever there are people, there will eventually be sex, no matter how bizarre the conditions, and one day as a result, no doubt, a child will be born in space. There would be physical obstacles to overcome: for instance, extra-terrestrial flight is known to be particularly hard on the kidneys, which rely on gravity to an extent, as do many of the body's other mechanisms.

But where there is a will, there is a way. There has been specu-lation that two Russian cosmonauts, Valeri Polyakov and Elena Kondakova, have already achieved the, um, delicate docking manoeuvre and, interestingly enough, Polyakov was to have been a technical consultant for *The Mark of Cassandra*.

With astonishing foresight, Elaine Lerner, who purports to be a Sunday School teacher from New England, has patented a contraption known as a 'belt to paradise' – which was designed to facilitate microgravitational sex. Apparently this thing has a great many straps and loops, comes in a 'red-satin look' or the 'black-leather look' and reminded one reviewer of a horse's har-ness ... although he acknowledged that for some this may be a good thing. Ms Lerner has apparently been attempting to interest NASA in her invention, although the idea of a professional astronaut

– radiation-deflecting spacesuit and all – wearing a red-satin device sounds like nothing so much as putting lipstick on a gorilla. The point is that our imaginations make sex an infinitely big deal but, in fact, what could be more mundane? It's one of the few things that everyone on Earth has in common.

On a political level, what people are doing in space has changed since Mir came down. Its successor, the International Space Station, is what it sounds like: a multinational endeavour, led by the Americans but with financial and scientific contributions from many other states. Similarly, the European Space Agency has seventeen member nations and a budget of £5.9 billion to last it until 2010 – but there's much talk these days of how public enthusiasm for space programmes is waning, largely because nothing has been attempted recently that grabs the imagination. People like manned missions to places they have heard of, and anything less, it seems, is boring.

The American budget for space dwarfs that of any country in Europe these days – underlining the extent to which the space race is a dash for territory in much the same way that 18th-century colonialism was. Whereas the European Space Agency has £5.9 billion for five years, NASA received £9.5 billion for 2006 alone. But that is just the tip of the iceberg. The US military budget for space is £17–23 billion a year, and speculation about what they need it for is fertile ground for conspiracy theorists.

For instance, the carrying case for the Hubble telescope broke before the device could be sent into orbit. There was pandemonium until it became clear that the US military could provide another – despite having no obvious reason for possessing it.

The space programmes of the former Soviet Union, the Chinese (they sent their first human 'taikonaut' into space in 2003) and the US military have this in common: the decision-making processes that created them were highly authoritarian. When democracy intervenes, money and impetus leak away from space projects. For this reason, it seems highly unlikely that the European Space Agency with its seventeen member states will ever have much of a role in pushing back the final frontier ...

But perhaps for this particular project, it's enough simply to be involved.

# There is an archway in Rome that Jews are forbidden by the Talmud to walk through

It was AD 66 and the Roman Empire was on formidable form. Judea – an area now divided between Israel, the West Bank and Jordan – had been an imperial province for 60 years, although it hadn't exactly been a pushover for the Romans.

Intellectually formed by a culture of rabbinical debate and discussion, the Jews were not inclined to roll over for anyone, at the point of a sword or otherwise – even if it also meant sanitation, security and good roads.

Perhaps the governors of that province had been a little crueller than elsewhere, or perhaps the history of dissent and the powerful local belief in a single divine authority made conquering the place more difficult than it had been to take over the rest of the Empire. Both are probably true – the one because of the other.

In that year, though, there was an uprising in Judea that changed the course of world history.

A general named Vespasian was sent to the dusty province by the Emperor Nero, accompanied by four Roman legions and his own son, a young man called Titus, and they set about quelling the uprising.

It wasn't easy. Like a New Testament version of the fairground game in which moles pop out of holes until you boink them on the head, every time the Romans dealt with one city, another became a problem. And then once they subdued a city, it was a question of keeping it that way. The engagement was long and more than usually bloody, even for an empire built on naked brutality.

The conquest took a lot of time and effort and many deaths – but the Romans knew all about killing and they dominated Europe, North Africa and the Middle East because of it.

To understand what animates an empire, today we are inclined to do what Woodward and Bernstein did after the break-in at the Watergate Hotel and 'follow the money'.

But ancient historians didn't write about economics. Money might be there as a motive if you read between the lines, but Josephus and Tacitus wrote of glory, conquest and tribute as the reasons why men went to distant places, faced death and killed people.

These explanations are, in many men's minds, their own reward. Money can't buy love, but power often wins it. Emperors frequently got murdered, but what they did in life echoed in eternity, as Ridley Scott suggested in *Gladiator*.

In the history books of the time, no Roman ever says, 'let's go to Judea because it's got oil' – olive oil, that is. Today we explain everything with economics because it's the tool that we have: it's Karl Marx's terrifying materialist legacy to the world. But you don't find it in Thucydides.

In those days, if you wanted someone to do your work for you, instead of invading another state, selling its natural resources and using the money, you simply went there and took slaves. The advantages of conquering your neighbours were so obvious that historians of that age didn't have to explain them. There were no competing theories about motivation.

But there was strong opposition to the Romans among the people of Judea. The men leading the rebellion were Zealots, who believed that only a Jewish king should rule their land. Their single-mindedness made the usual Roman approach to conquered populations – a short, sharp shock, followed by bread and circuses – impossible to sustain, because they simply were not interested. They were fanatics.

The Romans were desperate to undermine Jewish identity in the province and needed to do so to have any hope of a peaceful jurisdiction afterwards – and there was this temple …

It was the same temple that Jesus had stomped through a decade or so earlier, taking issue with the money-lenders, overturning tables and shouting about usury. If you wanted to really get people's attention in Judea, the Temple Mount was the place to go. It was the heart of the Jewish faith and – even though it no longer physically exists – for many, it still is.

There is only one place in the world where the Jews built the Temple: each place of worship apart from Temple Mount is just walls surrounded by empty space in comparison. Built by Solomon, destroyed by the Babylonians, rebuilt by the Jews on their return from Babylon, and then given a facelift by Herod: it was unlike ordinary synagogues in that the presence of the divine was said to be palpable.

Inside its walls was the Holy of Holies. God didn't exactly live there – the Hebrew God was too sophisticated for a temporal home. But his spirit had been known to put in an appearance from time to time.

By late summer AD 70, the Emperor Nero had died and been replaced by Vespasian, leaving Titus in charge of the Judean campaign. It was also at this point that the historian Josephus really came into his own.

He was in Jerusalem for the showdown between the Romans and the insurgents. In *The Jewish War*, he describes the ebb and flow of that battle in incredible detail. To read it is to appreciate that some things never change. People run up and down ravines. Small boys play tricks on the Romans. Women and children get killed – you can almost hear their cries.

Rome had the upper hand, though. When the fighting was over, the Temple was destroyed, as was most of Jerusalem. Titus left only three pillars standing as a memorial and razed everything else. Today, archaeologists in Jerusalem still find ashes believed to be from that period.

The Aggadah, a Jewish religious manuscript, contains a piece of propaganda describing how Titus desecrated the Holy of Holies after taking the Temple. He went there, sword in hand, it says, with two whores and had intercourse on the altar. On leaving, he is said to have raised his bloodied sword, shouting that he had killed God.

On his return to Rome he was feted: his father was the Emperor (as he became himself a decade later), and the three-day celebrations are commemorated by the Arcus Titi – the Arch of Titus – which still stands at one end of the Via Sacra.

It looks like a smaller, more intricate and far older version of the Arc de Triomphe. Images in bas-relief on its inside show the destruction of the Temple, the pillaging of its contents and the triumphal return to Rome of Titus.

Josephus estimates that 1.1 million Jews were killed during the uprising; Tacitus says 600,000. Between these two figures reverberates the fact that nobody was really counting.

Even in the 1st century AD, it's possible that there were more Jews in Rome than there were in Jerusalem; when the Arch was built, Jewish elders forbade all Hebrews from walking through it. In the Middle Ages, Jewish travellers would pay to pass through a neighbouring house rather than walk through something that commemorated the submission of their race and the destruction of the Temple – which has never been rebuilt.

This stricture eventually appeared in the Talmud, which was compiled around AD 600, by which time Rome had conquered Palestine, sending a Jewish diaspora half way around the world.

But without the destruction of the Temple – on whose site the Islamic Dome of the Rock now stands – Judaism wouldn't be what it is. Ironically, by destroying the physical heart of the Jewish faith, the Romans freed it from its geographical location – making it a world religion that travelled unencumbered by anything except memories. By killing Judaism's hearth gods, the Romans unintentionally gave it spirituality. But they also burned Jerusalem to the ground in a war for a city that continues to this day.

# For the last ten years the EU's auditors have refused to approve its accounts

Edward Leigh MP, the chairman of the House of Commons Public Accounts Committee (PAC), had hidden his slippers behind a chair. He is the man to speak to about fraud in the public sector and he had changed out of his comfortable footwear in order to do so. I didn't want him to be uncomfortable, but there was the small matter of a missing £629 million …

In 2003 the EU's budget was £67.2 billion. In that same year the European Anti-Fraud Office (OLAF) put reported fraud at £629 million, or slightly less than 1 per cent of the overall budget, which sounds terrible.

The European Court of Auditors has had the job of scrutinising the EU's accounts since 1994, in the same way that Arthur Andersen or PricewaterhouseCoopers might do for a large business. But it's been unable to approve the accounts – 'sign them off' – because they contain large holes.

If the European Union was a business that couldn't get its accounts signed off, it would have negative reports in the financial pages of newspapers, its stock would plummet, the cost of borrowing money would increase and its lines of credit would probably dry up. It would be a dead EU. The fact that none of these things has taken place is a measure of how different the public sector is from the private.

The National Audit Office (NAO) does a similar job to the European Court of Auditors. It scrutinises British public finances and decides whether the taxpayer is getting value for money. The PAC, composed of MPs, then oversees the NAO. And because Britain contributed £6.8 billion to the EU in 2003 and got only £4.1 billion back again, for farmers and so on, it was the EU's second-largest net contributor after Germany.

British taxpayers' money is being spent in Brussels, so the NAO and the PAC hold their own hearings and write their own reports about the EU's finances. The PAC holds the NAO to account and they both do the honours for the European Court of Auditors.

## DID DAVID HASSELHOFF END THE COLD WAR?

Edward Leigh, of the slippers, has been the chairman of the PAC since October 2001. His beautiful office with its river view sits magisterially on the committee-room floor of the House of Commons, and contains a picture of Charles de Gaulle balanced on a shelf in the corner. This may well be irony because he is a Tory Eurosceptic. He has a florid complexion and unusually vivid features that wouldn't look entirely out of place in the National Portrait Gallery – 'English country squire, circa 1700'. He is also approachable and personable, which are qualities not always found in an elected representative, in my experience.

The subject for discussion was whether EU fraud is as bad as it appears to be. Since Mr Leigh routinely deals with public money and the various ways in which it gets pilfered, squandered and lost, he is one of a handful of people who has a context in which to place the subject.

So, failing to have one's accounts signed off for ten years sounds pretty bad. Is it, I asked? 'Well, it is and it isn't', he said. 'It sounds awful, but ... Yes, it basically means that the whole thing is out of control to a greater or lesser extent. It means they [the EU] can't justify all their items of expenditure.'

In particular, the Common Agricultural Policy (CAP) and the Structural Fund (which targets poor areas within the EU) have been singled out as culprits in terms of fraud, corruption and waste.

'But', he said, 'bear in mind that our own National Audit Office has been unable to sign off the accounts of the Department of Work and Pensions – which is in the Department of Social Security in Whitehall – for thirteen years to the tune of about £4 billion a year.'

Since the overall budget for the British government in 2003 was £419.1 billion, this represents about the same percentage of the British budget as the EU's fraud does: slightly more, in fact. If Mr Leigh appeared underwhelmed by the EU playing fast and loose with taxpayers' money it was because he had seen it before.

'Look', he said. 'You don't have to be a Eurosceptic to see that the European Union is a very weakly-run organisation. But it is an international organisation and they always suffer these problems in spades. Look at the UN. There is a lack of accountability because there is a lack of interest. Apart from politicians, who has ever heard of the European Court of Auditors ... who cares? Of course, we should care because it is our money. We should care.' By 'we', he obviously means the general public because it was clear that he does care … sometimes, at least.

He added: 'But the trouble is that there is no political will to make the EU more accountable. Some of the reported fraud is British, obviously, and we don't really want the European Court of Auditors or some bureaucrat from Europe chasing the money back here, all the way to a farm gate in Yorkshire.'

Do we not?

'Well, it would be a huge extension of the power of the EU. It would become much more like a government and I don't think any political party with the possible exception of the Liberals would want that. So to be fair to the EU, they are a bit stuck. They are made to seem incompetent because the individual nations will not give them the jurisdiction to follow their own money.'

Things have reached this point, he explained, for a whole host of reasons. Firstly, press releases on the subject go unreported by newspapers across Europe, just as they do in Britain, because when something happens for several years in a row it becomes the status quo. Newspapers don't run the story because it's regarded as boring, European taxpayers aren't outraged because they have forgotten about it, so they don't force their governments to act. Who in western Europe campaigns for fiscal prudence … except Gordon Brown? (Although, admittedly, it seems to work for him, so perhaps there's a lesson in there somewhere.)

Secondly, complexity is an issue. Many of the forms that farmers in particular have to fill in are rather baroque (and the CAP is more than 40 per cent of the total EU budget). The forms were designed as compromises between nations with different farming regimes. Small and politically significant French and German farms contrast with British agribusiness, which doesn't really need the subsidies. However, without these subsidies, the British would challenge the Germans as the EU's largest net contributor.

The forms can't be simplified because the compromises they involve took so long to arrive at in the first place. So we are left with a process that causes genuine mistakes and allows fraud to pass unnoticed in a blur of boxes to tick, columns of figures and unchallenged statistics.

Thirdly, the EU hands out most subsidies at a national level. This creates problems because different countries have varying levels of probity in their public accounting, but no country has any jurisdiction to look at the accounts of any other.

And fourthly, although similar in function to the British National Audit Office, the European Court of Auditors doesn't have a powerful political committee – such as the PAC – to oversee its actions. The European Parliament remains weak for the political convenience of the member states.

The reasoning goes something like this: 'It would be less wasteful of taxpayers' money to allow the EU to follow its own money properly. But to make that possible would involve giving the EU a legitimacy that would make it look like a serious challenger to national governments. So let's not rock the boat.'

The EU and the British government have similar levels of fraud and corruption, yet the EU has the handicap of working without proper oversight. Perhaps there's a reason why national governments don't want to see the EU improving vigilance and reducing fraud?

# Next to the former Berlin Wall, two neighbours resolved their argument about a garden ... by dividing it with a wall

Osman Kalin immigrated to Germany from Anatolia in Turkey. Like many of his compatriots, he had travelled north to Berlin in search of a better life. In 1984, he was living in the Berlin-Kreuzberg district of the city behind the Marianna Platz, where every 1 May police and demonstrators traditionally gathered for their annual, anti-capitalist riot.

Perhaps it was becoming a habit for him – looking for the next improvement – because one day he noticed, as he gazed across the road, that the plot of land opposite was not being put to any use. A shame, he thought, because land was always handy ... even if this parcel of it was within spitting distance of the wall that gashed Berlin.

He asked around. 'Who owned the land?', he wondered to his neighbours, but they didn't know. So Osman, being a resourceful person, took the initiative.

He began by clearing away several square feet of rubbish that looked as if it had been there so long it had taken root. And when he examined the soil he realised that it had real promise – he had a farming background.

So he finished the clean-up job and began to plant. He sowed flowers, sweet potatoes, onions, and apricot and cherry trees. He started selling some of the potatoes at the nearby Maybachufer market, taking them there on a trolley that he built for the purpose.

Then he grew ambitious. Before too long there was a fine-looking summerhouse, made from recycled materials, standing alongside the garden. It had no electricity and no running water, but wisteria and sweet peas tumbled down its walls until it looked of a piece with the rest of his garden. He could sit on his porch made of reclaimed wood and enjoy the view he had engineered.

87

Then one day he received a visit from two young men with automatic weapons. They looked unfamiliar because they were from the other side of the wall. 'What are you doing with this land?' they demanded. 'Whose is it?' 'It's mine', said Osman, who, after his hard work, felt entitled to say this with some pride.

'No. It's not yours', they snapped back. 'It belongs to the GDR.' This surprised the old Turk, since his plot was on the wrong side of the wall for this to be true: he was in the West. But although they looked perplexed at the dilemma he presented, the soldiers left him alone and didn't come back.

A detailed political map of the area, like that kept by Hermann Koch (former chief cartographer of the German Democratic Republic (GDR)) in his now-famous archive of material relating to the Wall, shows that the land Osman Kalin cultivated is an odd historical kink.

Somehow – and there were a few places like this – a triangle of land that belonged to the Soviet-controlled East Germany ended up on the wrong side of the wall, explaining why it had stood unused for so long. But both GDR and West German authorities turned a blind eye to the garden and the summerhouse, although they had been thrown up without planning permission, and Osman Kalin became a minor local celebrity.

People would stop by and say hello. Osman opened a small café where tourists could sit down and have a coffee. Journalists came to interview him.

Then one day his neighbour Mustapha Akyol, who had followed Osman's example and begun to cultivate nearby, pointed out that some of the onions he had planted had mysteriously ended up on Osman's patch.

No, no: that was not the case, insisted Osman. They were, in fact, his onions and anybody who knew the land they worked would know this. Mustapha disagreed. There was a fight and blows were exchanged.

Soon afterwards visitors to the area – for the Wall had come down by now and there was a sentimental yen to see where East had met West – were surprised to notice that a roll of wire netting had been run straight across what had previously been an open piece of land, separating the plots. The angry neighbours had built their own wall.

Whether you are inclined to giggle or be impressed by the heavy-handed nature of the metaphor in this true story, the implications are rather depressing.

As a form of conflict resolution, building a wall to divide two areas has always left a lot to be desired. From Belfast in Northern Ireland, where some streets were blocked off to separate Catholics from Protestants, to Israel with its huge wall designed to make life more difficult for suicide bombers, such rulings have always been temporary physical solutions to problems that exist inside people's minds.

'United we stand, divided we fall', goes the motto. Cutting things into pieces, whatever Quentin Tarantino may say about the balletic nature of violence, is most frequently the opposite of a creative act.

The Berlin Wall, as a hard fact and as an idea, haunted the early years of many people my age (I was born in 1970). It was symbolic of the big story in our lives, the thing over which we had no control, over which nobody had any control: the mushroom cloud of our collective imaginations.

Our worst fear was that at any moment we all could be vaporised. And the name given to our failsafe mechanism, the reason why it wouldn't happen, was the least reassuring name you could imagine: MAD or mutually assured destruction. It was the theory that neither of the world's two superpowers would launch a nuclear attack on the other, because the time lapse between launching a missile and its detonation would inevitably lead to their own annihilation … Great. *This* was what the adults had come up with – the big idea lurking behind the arms race and brinkmanship that appeared every night in some form on the news. It was psychotic, in that it was so profoundly relevant to our everyday lives that the only way to manage it was to pretend that it didn't exist.

But it was pervasive and often became a metaphor for the condition of our lives. Post-apocalyptic stories were everywhere. On television, Anthony Andrews (the beautiful Sebastian in *Brideshead Revisited*) took a turn as a Catweazle-style naked mad-man in the 1984 nightmare about the last surviving humans in a blasted landscape, called *Z for Zachariah*. *Battlestar Galactica* was made possible because we believed that the world could come to an end through human fault and that it was perfectly plausible that the survivors would have to set out to find somewhere 'clean' to live. And it was always only a question of time before Sylvester Stallone used *Rocky* as a vehicle for a US-Soviet clash. It was the biggest story on the planet.

As a youngster, I was mildly traumatised by the Raymond Briggs book *When the Wind Blows*. My parents bought this, having been fans of *Fungus the Bogeyman*, but hid it when they realised it was all about the death by radiation of an ordinary couple after a nuclear war. My sister and I found it anyway.

*War Games* with Matthew Broderick, *Einstein's Monsters* by Martin Amis, *Riddley Walker* by Russell Hoban, even the song 'Hammer to Fall' by Queen – referred directly to the appalling threat under which we conducted our lives. There was a kind of crushing force to the whole thing that the subsequent War on Terror has so far been unable even vaguely to replicate – though not for want of trying. Suicide bombings might result in the deaths of an unlucky handful who were in the wrong place at the wrong time. But one nuclear weapon could have vaporised the entire city of Norwich, where we lived for a time and which was surrounded by American airforce bases, making it a likely target. There were no circumstances under which being observant would have made a difference. There was no illusion of control.

I remember, much earlier and in a different town, my mum, fresh from the only Campaign for Nuclear Disarmament rally she ever attended, hurling herself to the floor of the front room, shouting: 'It's the end of the world!' The cause of this was a V of low-flying jets,
roaring low over our north London home on their way to a fly-past for the Queen's birthday. Seeing your mum dive under a sofa because she feels powerless to do anything else leaves a big impression on a young mind.

The story of Osman Kalin and Mustapha Akyol isn't an optimistic one. It seems that they let themselves down by falling for somebody else's trick. But also, you get the sneaking suspicion that the seeds of this particular problem may be in all of us. As strangers in a strange land, they represented a fresh start but still messed it up. At least the bigger wall in the story no longer casts the kind of psychological shadow that it once did.

# Finnish food is better than French food

At the beginning of July 2005, President Jacques Chirac of France was overheard explaining to President Putin of Russia and Chancellor Schröder of Germany why the British couldn't be trusted. 'They have the worst cuisine in the world. Except for Finland', he chuckled, unaware that a reporter had overheard his undiplomatic aside.

M Chirac, bless him, had put his foot in his mouth – it was a faux pas on the scale of one of those state-sponsored, architectural behemoths on which the French are so keen. But any hurt British feelings received swift compensation when the International Olympic Committee awarded the 2012 Games to London ahead of the favourite, Paris, a couple of days later. A coincidence? By all accounts there was only a wafer between London and Paris towards the end and there were two Finns on the committee, so draw your own conclusions.

But what were Chirac's remarks really all about? Is it possible that he actually believes that there is a connection between trustworthiness and how well one can cook? Anglo-French rivalry is an old story, but what could Finland of all places possibly have done to offend the palate of Monsieur Chirac?

'I was very surprised', said Petri Tuomi-Nikula, a Finnish diplomat based in London. 'Back in 1999, when Finland had the EU presidency, I met President Chirac. I had been responsible for organising a conference and he came to Finland as our guest.'

'I say I am surprised because he went much, much further than he really had to and thanked me effusively for the hospitality, singling the food out for a special mention. So ...', and the diplomat did a passable impression of a Gallic shrug. 'Who knows what it means?' All of which is further proof that these days it's not hard to be more diplomatic than the French, who appear to have been rather letting themselves go in this respect.

Once upon a time France was a world power. Theirs was the language of diplomacy, the arts, of high culture. Any well-educated person spoke it – it was the lingua franca of the *bien-pensant*. To this day, diplomats would say in English that, for instance, a *coup* brought about a *regime* change, followed by *rapprochement* and finally an *entente cordiale*. Similarly, it's hard to talk about a country's cuisine without using French terms. The culinary dictionary is littered with linguistic reminders of the French obsession with gastronomy.

But to be fair to *les rosbifs*, in recent years Britain, and specifically London, has also developed a reputation for good eating, partly because of the eclecticism of the city's population. Name a country and you will find a corresponding restaurant tucked away in Bloomsbury, Fitzrovia or Belgravia, quietly playing host to some of the millions of conversations, business transactions and cross-cultural gambits that have built the capital's global reputation. But – strangely, you might well think – there is no Finnish restaurant.

So my investigations had to take me farther afield. Relentless sleuthing in the eateries and cafés of Finland, solely in the service of this book, you understand, have led me to the opinion that there are several reasons for the absence of a Finnish culinary oeuvre abroad and the lack of any Finnish defence of their national table when it was attacked.

For a start, going to restaurants is a comparatively new idea for the Finns. They have been trying to get used to it since they officially became 'European' in 1995 when they joined the EU, and in this sense they can't compete with the French. In a country where more than 95 per cent of the population is officially Lutheran (the religious equivalent of a bucket of ice-cold water down the back), the most decadent thing one could do would be to drink a latte in a taxi on the way to a restaurant – because none of these things is, strictly speaking, *necessary*. The Finns do have a great national tradition of coffee drinking, right down to customs about who at the table should receive the first cup. But the scorn that the older generation reserves for the new-fangled, frothy Italian concoctions that have recently invaded the coffee shops of Helsinki is matched only by their undying passion for public transport, and their view that spending money in a restaurant is a stupid waste of one's hard-earned cash.

Joy, you see, is something that most Finns seem to need permission to experience, which is one of the reasons that it's such a great country to visit. You get the sense that your mere presence provides an excuse they wouldn't otherwise have to go a bit mad and, say, jump into your taxi on the way to a bar.

But none of this is to suggest that the Finns don't eat well. They do. It's just that it takes place in the privacy of their homes and, for the 80 per cent of them who have a second home, at their summer cottages among the trees and sweetwater lakes where most of their best fresh ingredients are to be found.

The summer cottages are, at heart, a very elaborate exercise in camping. They quite frequently have no plumbed-in toilet but, in a charming reversal of most people's priorities, it would be highly unusual to come across one without a sauna. The Finns leave their souls in these places, where they go to fish, hunt elk and pick mushrooms and berries from the forests that cover 65 per cent of Finland. Then they slow-cook and eat the results in a setting that makes their own kind of sense.

Crucially, the other relevant national trait here is modesty – which they possess to a degree that is actually confusing for an averagely astute non-Finn. For instance, my introduction to summer cottages came from a man who told me beforehand that it would be unwise to generalise from the oncoming experience because his was a very poor, mean version of a summer cottage. On arrival, I was confronted with a beautiful, candle-lit, wooden palace filled with 18th-century furniture, professionally carved statuary and a baby grand piano. It took one of my fellow guests to point out at the end of the evening that it was the owner's modesty that led him to, um, *lie* to me.

Similarly, it would have been out of character for the Finns to have pointed out after Chirac's remarks that his sentiment represented the height of ingratitude for the sumptuous hospitality he had received from the Finnish government on each of his several visits to their country. Moreover, Chirac probably knew this, making the Finns an easy target. As a modest people, they sometimes need others to speak up on their behalf.

It's true that in the 'Land of the Midnight Sun', where the vegetable-growing season is limited to only three months of the year, the bedtime snacks have very little greengrocery going on. But a trip to the herring fair in Helsinki in early October clarified the fundamental distinction between a meal in a French restaurant and soul food for minus forty degrees, Finnish-style.

Takeaway stalls on the quayside exerted a kind of slack-jawed traction on their customers, drawing them towards the potato dogs (sausages wrapped in a case of buttery, spiced potato); salmon soup with potatoes and dill; vendes (small herring) with garlic sauce; deep-fried pike balls; smoked salmon with blue cheese; eggy apple cake with cinnamon and cardamom served with sour cream; and vorschmack, which is lamb and beef spiced with herring and cooked for twelve hours: a hangover cure for the vodka belt, if ever there was one. People stood next to the Baltic, which was like a mill pond, hands and mouths shining with the glow-fried seafood and other glories that they were eating with their fingers. This – and not restaurants – is what Finnish food is all about.

So where did Chirac get off being so casually rude on a subject to which he had clearly given very little thought? It goes straight to the heart of the French worldview. They like to believe that, even if they are no longer a world power in political terms, they still have better food than everybody else. The French maintain a kind of cultural imperialism: indeed, it's at the epicentre of their national self-image and pride (which, as any good Lutheran would tell you, is a mortal sin). They believe in their gastronomic elitism so sincerely and have said so at such great length and in so many different contexts that the rest of the world, after a good feed, has frequently believed them – leading otherwise sane non-French people to act as mouthpieces for their Gallic culinary 'masters'.

The tradition is largely tied up with the life's work of Auguste Escoffier, the Frenchman who, in the late 19th and early 20th centuries, codified the most popular cooking techniques of his day, becoming the central authority on catering college syllabuses the world over. In this sense he is the single greatest figure at the heart of what's best termed 'French culinary colonialism' – part of a habit they have of appropriating universal techniques and labelling them 'French'.

But Escoffier worked at the Savoy in London for many years and for a German shipping line, as well as for several other places outside France. In his books, he elaborated on techniques that he'd come across all over Europe. So to claim his life's work as something uniquely French is like saying that the internet is British because Sir Tim Berners-Lee invented hypertext, or that Napoleon Bonaparte invented the law because he wrote it down. Personally, I've never had a good meal in Paris but I've probably simply been unlucky and – unlike Chirac – I am prepared to give the French the benefit of the doubt.

A meal can't be separated from its context: the people, the place and the mood. And Finnish food, like much else about the country, is simple, unostentatious, wholesome fare. Ultimately, though, the reason why I'd choose Finnish food over French, is because in Helsinki one is far less likely than in Paris to end up sharing a restaurant and therefore a meal with Jacques Chirac – a man whose rudeness (in his own, food-obsessed terms) towards his former Finnish hosts has known no bounds.

# Europeans work 350 hours fewer a year than Americans

Europeans can take a certain comfort in this statistic: the United States might be the world's only remaining superpower, but at least it has to work for it.

The Organization for Economic Cooperation and Development specialises in producing these kinds of numbers, which by their nature are averages. In fact, Iceland, the Czech Republic and Switzerland all put in more hours in a year than America, but the rest of us drag the average down. Belgium, the Netherlands and France are the most productive European countries in terms of output per hours worked, showing that there is a difference between quality and quantity when it comes to time spent at a desk. Germany, Ireland and Italy are also ahead of the United States in this respect.

But on total output per capita the US comes out ahead, because the average European takes five or six weeks holiday a year, whereas Americans get only two weeks off (and have no legal right to a holiday at all). Europe's total overall productivity is between 92 and 97 per cent of the US level, depending on how you read the figures.

Back in the early 1970s, Europe and the United States were about equal in terms of the number of hours worked, holidays taken and per capita income. But as productivity in both places increased, Americans chose to take the extra as money to spend on consumer goods, whereas Europeans opted for extra holidays. This is why Europe's income per capita is now roughly only 72 per cent of America's.

These differences between the two workplace cultures represent two different approaches to life. In terms of attitudes to work, Britain falls somewhere in the middle, which is surprising considering how much of the rest of our cultural life is American in origin. It's easy to forget the differences.

The difference between the two continents is greatest at the lower end of the pay scale. Professional people tend to be paid a salary to do a job; the time this takes doesn't matter so much to their employer, so long as the job gets done. Granted, there are cultural pressures to put in longer hours at all levels of US society, but unskilled workers there are driven to do this by financial necessity. The pressures on them are different to those on European workers.

In the United States, there's no minimum wage, meaning that companies are free to compete with each other by cutting their wage bills and hourly rates – constrained only by the consideration that the lower the wages the harder it is to find good employees. Also, because there's no health safety net, people on low wages need to work longer in order to buy health insurance for themselves and their families. There is an imperative attached to this that comparatively few Europeans experience, involving fear.

Fewer workplace regulations in the US mean that 24-hour opening for supermarkets, restaurants and bars isn't unusual, especially in cities, making it possible to work all the hours that God sends if you want or need to.

But there's also a much stronger belief in the US that if you work hard, it's possible to change your station in life and get the things for your children that you never had yourself. There's a large body of economic research suggesting that the evidence supporting this belief isn't as strong as the belief itself. But still, it gives you a spiritual reason to push on through, as you do your twelve-hour shift in an abattoir, bartend for drunks in the middle of the night, or serve a Big Mac and fries to an obese insomniac.

Europeans, by contrast, are far more inclined to be grumpy about their social station, generally believing that their life chances are circumscribed by who their parents are, where they were born and a whole host of things over which they have no control.

In an attempt to even up the perception of unfairness, unions have more of a foothold in Europe than in the US. And as a result of Europe's corresponding emphasis on workers' rights, the French government, for instance, created the experimental 35-hour week.

In a paper called 'Work and Leisure in Europe', some Harvard academics recently suggested that unionisation and workplace regulations over a long period have been responsible for the apparent European 'cultural tendency towards leisure'. Why so different on either side of the Atlantic?

They pointed out that as a society's working hours go down, the enthusiasm for working fewer hours increases. Since Europe and the US were in very similar positions until the early seventies, it's hard to argue that Europeans simply have a cultural predisposition to go to sleep under a tree. Instead, they said, people enjoy their time off more when they can spend it with their friends and family. Government-enforced regulations about working hours act as a 'social multiplier' because people are inherently social creatures.

By this token it seems likely that Americans would also enjoy more leisure time if they had the opportunity to take it in a co-ordinated way. It may be simply the lack of regulation of their own working environments that prevents them from taking time off, even though they have greater individual flexibility about their hours. There's little point taking time off on the weekends, after all, if your friends and family will be working anyway.

Judging success by just one measure is rarely wise. Americans may work more hours and have more money, but they are also increasingly unhealthy – because of a culture of convenience made necessary by their lack of leisure time. Why would you choose to eat a Big Mac if you had the time to enjoy a long meal with friends?

Similarly, using money as the sole measure of a nation's worth or value is a bit short-sighted. The late US Senator Robert Kennedy put it like this:

'The Gross National Product includes air pollution and advertising for cigarettes and ambulances to clear the highways of carnage. It counts special locks for our doors and jails for the people who break them. GNP includes the destruction of the redwoods and the death of Lake Superior. It grows with the production of napalm and missiles and nuclear warheads … it doesn't allow for the health of our families, the quality of their education, or the joy of their play. It is indifferent to the decency of our factories and the safety of our streets alike. It does not include the beauty of our poetry, or the strength of our marriages, or the intelligence of our public debate, or the integrity of our public officials … it measures everything, in short, except that which makes life worthwhile.'

Another US Senator and presidential hopeful, Paul Tsongas, pointed out: 'No man ever said on his deathbed, "I wish I had spent more time at the office".'

DID DAVID HASSELHOFF END THE COLD WAR?

The ways of measuring international business competitiveness are interesting in their own right. But there comes a point where you have to ask – competition for what? Europe may have a less successful economy than the United States in purely monetary terms, but can you put a price on happiness?

# Santa Claus lives in Greenland and he is broke

Father Christmas is a capitalist construction, ho ho ho! The jovial fat man, with the red-and-white outfit and billowy beard, was designed by Coca-Cola for a marketing campaign in 1938. Before that, he was equally likely to appear as a friendly fellow in green, or a magician-ish man with a long blue robe and a twinkle in his eye. So a discussion of his financial affairs isn't entirely unfamiliar to the spirit of Christmas.

Greenland has had a long association with Santa Claus. In 1934, Walt Disney produced a cartoon called *Santa's Journey*, in which Donald Duck, together with Huey, Louis and Dewey, travelled through Greenland to the North Pole to meet the great man. Along the way they met Eskimos and polar bears and generally helped to create a mythical Christmas theme that has been popular ever since. For this, the Greenlandic tourist board, such as it is, is grateful.

The cartoon was seen all over the world, and soon afterwards letters addressed to Santa Claus began arriving in Greenland, which was a colony of Denmark at the time. The letters wound up at the only business then operating, the Royal Greenlandic Trading Company, which was owned by the Danish government. The company's employees began answering children's letters voluntarily and this became a tradition, although one that was financially manageable only with the backing of a large company.

Greenland got home rule in 1977, but it has remained dependent on Denmark for about 60 per cent of its Gross Domestic Product (GDP), as well as for its education, healthcare, foreign and defence policies. But then, only 56,000 people live on the vast expanse of Arctic tundra, along with a few hundred polar bears, rather more seals and some reindeer. Every person in Greenland is subsidised to the tune of around £7,000 a year by the Danish taxpayer.

It's a place where there are no roads between towns and it's not uncommon for a middle-ranking government employee to have his own helipad through need rather than ostentation. Most transport is managed by water and the country is much closer to Canada than it is to Denmark. Nonetheless, it joined the European Community in

1972 at the same time as Denmark, and only withdrew in 1985 after a controversy over fishing quotas. It remains the only country to have withdrawn from the European project.

These days, Greenland receives a large EU subsidy in return for fishing access to its chilly waters, although there's a strong sense that the deal is overly generous to Greenland and that the situation will soon change.

Around 50,000 letters addressed to Santa still arrive in Greenland each Christmas from all over the world, although the vast majority – around 45,000 – are from Denmark. After the official demise of Danish colonial rule, a company called Santa Claus of Greenland took over the job of answering these Christmas pleas. This company was an offshoot of Tele Greenland, owned by the Greenland Home Rule government, meaning that Santa Claus actually appeared as an item on Greenland's annual finance bill between 1991 and 2003.

But, sadly, by Christmas 2004, the company was forced to admit to the world that it could no longer respond to the thousands of children's letters, due to a government belt-tightening exercise. 'The coffers are empty', Lisa Johansen, aka 'Santa's helper', told the world's press. All public funds to Santa's foundation had been cut.

During the 1990s, the Greenlandic government had hoped that Santa Claus would be a good way to promote the country – to stimulate tourism and trade, raise the profile of the place, and firm up its national identity.

But there were structural difficulties. Getting European tourists to a place 4,000 miles away would always be expensive. The Danish government's monopoly of the one air service between Greenland and Copenhagen made matters worse, with tickets costing around £1,500 return. Without the political will to change this situation, tourism to Greenland remains at the 'adventurous' end of the international travel market. And unfortunately there's no civilian air service at all to Greenland from Canada: the only flights in that direction go to the US military base at Thule.

This isolation, more than anything else, places a limit on what Greenlanders can do for Santa and vice versa. But demoralisation really set in when the fishing industry – Greenland's only serious economic activity – went into recession in the late 1990s. And stiff competition has also emerged from Finland, which recently launched its own Santa attraction in Lapland. Meanwhile, piles of unanswered children's letters have rotted away and poor old Greenland Santa is kicking his rounded heels.

'I am the CEO and the President of Santa Claus of Greenland', said Anders Laesoe. He usually introduces himself as 'Santa's Best Friend', mainly, he explained, because it never fails to impress children. 'But I get no salary from the company and it has no employees. Santa is very poor these days. So I am paid by Tele Greenland and my Santa work is something that I have to do when I get home. We try to do things professionally, but it is hard. Our activities are getting smaller and smaller.'

He was very enthusiastic, but when he mentioned Finland's Santa take-over he sounded glum, like someone with their nose pressed against a brightly-lit window. The Finns have been hugely successful at attracting tourism at the luxury end of the market, offering jingling sleigh rides, snug family cottages in snowy woods and visits to Santa Claus in his 'own home'. By comparison, Santa has only a giant mailbox in Greenland – the largest in the world, it's claimed – but no visible means of support in this snowy clime.

Laesoe's words implied that if his Santa Claus belonged to Denmark rather than Greenland, he would probably be 'comfortable', rather than on the breadline. But Greenland is now an overseas country and territory on the EU's terms. It has a predominantly Inuit (Eskimo) population and suffers from a problem familiar to many colonised peoples: its economy is overly dependent on a few sources of income and isn't helped at all by its remote location and years of under-development.

For instance, although there's a tiny university in Greenland, at Ilisimatusarfik, it accepts only Greenlandic speakers as students and awards fewer than twenty degrees each year. A trickle of would-be graduates depart for Copenhagen, Stockholm or London but few ever return. Professional jobs in Greenland are mainly filled by Danish men and women.

'When Greenlanders get to Copenhagen they are often seen on the streets, lying around drunk. It is pretty similar to the Aboriginal situation in Australia. There are many who go there and are successful, but this isn't who most Danish people think of first. They are perceived as alcoholic and worthless', explained Mr Laesoe.

'And then in Greenland the problem is that they import people like me from Denmark, with degrees, to help them with higher-level jobs – but it produces resentment. They feel the Danish are monopolising all the good jobs but most Greenlanders are unqualified to do them.'

'There is a tendency towards racism against the Danish', he added. 'And violence.' He and his wife and children have been in Greenland for eight years – after seven you qualify for naturalisation – but his young son was recently beaten up by people who called him a 'Danish bastard'.

There is a possibility that Greenland might have been better off financially today if it had remained inside the European Union. Around five years after it left a whole range of 'structural funds' were created to address uneven distribution of wealth across EU countries. It may have qualified for funds to make companies including Santa Claus of Greenland a going concern, enabling the economy to diversify away from fishing. But that window of opportunity has now closed because in order to qualify, an area must have a GDP that is less than 75 per cent of the EU average. Denmark's considerable financial support for its former colony would probably lift it out of this bracket – especially since the arrival of the ten relatively poor new EU countries in 2004. Greenland's problems are very specific to itself.

So Santa Claus of Greenland has fallen upon hard times. If you run into him and his formerly well-filled red jacket looks a bit threadbare, shabby and loose around the middle, wish him a Merry Christmas. You might make his year.

# The last breeding pair of Maltese falcons was shot dead by hunters in 1982

Malta consists of five small islands that sit 60 miles south of Sicily, 220 miles north of Libya, and equidistant between Gibraltar and Alexandria. By its map reference (35°50′N 14°35′E) you may know it. But most of the creatures that find their way there do so without clocks or charts. This rocky outcropping, half the size of London, is directly under the flight path of many of Europe's migrating birds.

The Earth is slightly tilted on its axis. It wobbles as it goes around, meaning that although the planet spins on its pin once a day, any place on the globe finds itself at a different coordinate in space depending on the time of year. As a result we have seasons – for which many of us give thanks, since it is one of the natural graces of living somewhere without a Caribbean climate.

When it becomes too cold to sustain insect life in the tundra and boreal forests of northern Europe, birds are forced southwards, making their yearly migration to an area in which they can find food. They arrive to see the disappearing tails of other species that usually live there, and who are themselves heading further south for winter. Tundra birds have adapted to living off fewer calories than their more southerly cousins, meaning that they can happily over-winter in places where less food is available. In this way, wave upon wave of birds displace each other, whorling across the globe in spring and autumn. Their complex movements make human migration seem transparent by comparison.

We don't really know how the birds do it – get from A to B with such uncanny accuracy each year. One strong possibility is that it's related to the sun. A man called Gustav Kramer discovered, with the aid of a planetarium and some mirrors, that if you 'move' the sun, the trajectory of a bird's path will most often change by the same number of degrees. There is also speculation that some species can detect the Earth's magnetic field. Areas that have an anomalous field – such as the Bermuda Triangle – quite often have the same effect on birdlife as they do on man-made navigational devices and whales: they make them go loopy. Whales often end up on beaches in areas like this.

But whatever their methods, birds are hard-wired to know where they need to go each year: it isn't a learned experience for them. And some are luckier than others.

Pity the tired feathered migrant, for instance, who after hours of flapping across choppy open water, pitted against the weather, has the misfortune to stumble across the isles of Malta. With a population of 350,000, it is among the most densely inhabited places in the world – and its human numbers are swelled further by tourism, which is the country's main industry. More pertinently for the birds, an estimated 12,000-plus people on Malta enjoy hunting on a regular basis. Malta's history of bird hunting and trapping goes back centuries and is related to the sheer amount of birdlife formerly present there.

As many a startled tourist could tell you, Malta is a place for which the phrase 'crack of dawn' could have been invented. Not only do men (and sometimes women) feel free to shoot down anything that has feathers, but they quite often climb into boats and paddle offshore in order to get the clearest shots. Having Malta on your flight path is the bird world's equivalent of having to survive the D-Day landings twice a year.

Originally, hunting was a pastime of the nobility. In 1239, Emperor Frederick II annexed Malta to Sicily and then a year later, intrigued by reports of the island's copious bird life, he sent a team of eighteen falconers to investigate. It was the beginning of an enduring legend.

The peregrine falcon, of which Maltese falcons were a subspecies, has been a symbol of ferocious power and wealth for as long as mankind has had the energy to look upwards. They are raptors whose astonishing speed allows them to strike other birds with a ferocity that rarely fails – their diet includes pigeon, blackbird, duck and pheasant. They are the most successful bird of prey on the planet – 'peregrine' means widely dispersed, well-travelled or far-flung, as well as 'pilgrim'.

They can achieve speeds on a downward trajectory of up to 270 miles per hour. When they are preparing to strike, they clench their talons and plunge down on their oblivious quarry, usually knocking the bird unconscious with a single blow. The force of the impact is such that it may kill outright – then, as the victim falls, the falcon circles back, plucking its prey out of the air with its claws. If a bird survives the initial blow, the peregrine quickly breaks its neck with a strike from its powerful beak.

For many centuries, kings and emperors admired the ruthless efficiency of this lord of the skies and, since the peregrine proved surprisingly amenable to domestication, used it to practise the art of falconry.

In 1530, after the crusades, Charles V of France gave Malta to the Knights of St John as a base, in return for a nominal yearly rent of a falcon or hawk. It became customary thereafter for similar gifts to be presented to European royalty, and in this way the Maltese falcon became a legend enmeshed in the mythology of Mediterranean power games.

When Dashiell Hammett wrote his crime thriller *The Maltese Falcon*, he took the basic idea of the crusaders' tribute, but made the falcon itself a bejewelled trinket – so valuable that various unpleasant characters are prepared to lie and kill to own it. Humphrey Bogart played the morally bankrupt Sam Spade in the 1941 movie, and it is this film that has made the Maltese falcon an icon in the modern imagination. To Americans, it is something inscrutably European and valuable; and to Europeans, it is a now-extinct bird representing the ruthless pursuit of power.

So there was a certain poetic justice to how the Maltese falcon met its end. 'It last bred in the cliffs at Ta' Cenc in Gozo in 1982', said Joseph Mangion, chairman of Bird Life Malta. 'It is likely that the birds were shot illegally from sea craft in the same year.'

He explained how, for the sake of a day's shooting, the last Maltese falcons were turned into a puff of feathers over a cliff. They were wiped out by the democratisation of hunting on Malta that has made guns and refrigerators – for storing the dead bodies of your trophies before taxidermy – everyday household items. The Maltese falcons were overtaken by history.

Eighteen other species have also become extinct on Malta, the barn owl and jackdaw among them, and when Malta joined the EU in 2004, hunting was one of the major issues at stake. Malta now has strict legal guidelines, but the issue is really enforcement.

Hunting is so ingrained in the culture that Christmas nativity scenes quite often have a tiny figurine of a shooter stalking around the background of the stable – despite the fact that guns were not invented until 1,500 years after the birth of Christ.

Another favourite Maltese still-life is the collection of illegally-hunted rare birds, stuffed by one of the many part-time taxidermists, carefully reconstituted, and grouped together on a papier mâché rock or branch, as if in debate. They probably wouldn't be so popular if they were more realistic – with the birds arranged in the state in which they tumbled out of the air. Like some ghoulish Charles Addams cartoon, they would have bloody stumps where wings were, misshapen faces because their beaks were blown off, and far fewer legs than is generally considered to be normal.

The loss of the Maltese falcon is emblematic of an era in which, with a little money, we may all now live like kings. Unfortunately, in this instance it's the bird world that has suffered the consequences.

# There are 370 people who are banned from the EU

In the same way that it makes sense to ask 'what is the EU for?', the partner question would be 'what is the EU against?'. And there is a comprehensive list of undesirables that answers it.

The individuals and organisations on this list are representatives of the world's most corrupt, brutal and violent regimes and the terrorism that they frequently engender. Glancing through it brings back memories of all the news reports you have ever seen and would really like to forget.

It includes Liberians responsible for the deaths of 200,000 in two civil wars: Charles Taylor, a warlord given asylum by Nigeria, is on the list, as are men called Cyril Allen, Reginald B. Goodridge and Jenkins Dunbar – their curiously Victorian-sounding names echo their ancestors' lives as American slaves and returned freedmen.

The entire military government of Burma is present and corrupt. Burma has an estimated 70,000 child soldiers, forced labour is commonplace and a refusal to comply with the authorities often ends in torture, rape or murder – possibly all three. In Burma it is illegal to possess a telephone, fax machine, computer, modem or software, so the fact that this list even exists is a significant rebuke to the Burmese regime.

Next to them jostle the al-Qaida-style operatives and their financial backers who make up the bread and butter of our daily newspaper reportage. The Islamic names of these men, who are notable for their large number of aliases, invade our minds, terrorising us even over the breakfast table. These uniquely modern stories about suicide bombings and carefully laid plans for atrocities, even when foiled at the last moment, are still effective for terror. As a result of these men's hideous imaginations, we dwell on the one plot that may elude the security forces, devastating familiar places and killing people we love.

Scattered between these individual names are the organisations that support them: the shell-companies, 'charitable organisations' and state-owned enterprises that finance criminality and act as conduits for its money. They are named on this list so that accounts that deal with them can be spotted and reported. It includes the dull-sounding State Battery Manufacturing Enterprise of Myanmar (Burma), the Rafidain State Organisation for Irrigation Projects of Iraq, and an Al-Hamati Sweets Bakeries, whose purpose apparently extends a bit further than confectionery. These groups and around 2,500 others lurk there as a reminder that Gross Domestic Product isn't always a measure of well-being.

But it has to be said that the External Relations department of the European Commission doesn't make its 'consolidated list of people and entities' easy for one to read.

Weeks elapsed while I tried to get hold of a copy in a usable format, and finally, I failed. I ended up with a bad print-out of the list that I had to go and collect in person from the nearest European Commission office because my humble PC couldn't download it. Even then, it wasn't entirely clear how many people were on the list, because there were no labels explaining which of the names were real and which were aliases. Some guesswork was involved in arriving at the rough figure of 370.

The reason that ordinary people can't read this list is that it's formatted for software available only within large banking institutions. Making a PDF file for taxpayers wouldn't be hard, but evidently EU transparency doesn't extend that far. The list is available only for banks because it is intended only for them.

Contrast this approach with that of the United States. The US Treasury has a similar list online at www.treas.gov – with fifteen sub-headings naming the countries and international problems that their sanctions address. The sub-headings include diamond trading, the proliferation of weapons of mass destruction and narcotics trafficking, as well as Burma, Cuba and Iran. Each sub-heading contains a list of the people sought, the actions that the US is empowered to take and an overview of the subject. There is a separate list formatted for banks: the one on the website exists simply so that the public can see what their government is doing on its behalf. Browsing the website is clarity itself.

The contrast between the EU and the US lists illustrates two things. Firstly, that whatever the European Union says about its attitude to openness and transparency, these qualities are not among its institutional reflexes. While trying to read the list, I spoke to the EU press office in London, the external affairs press office in Brussels, and the office that produced the list of sanctions. I encountered a combination of unconcern that I couldn't read the document, irritation that I was persistent, and unhelpfulness from people who kept sending me web addresses for sites I couldn't open. Self-evidently, it's impossible to hold an institution to account if you can't even find out what it's doing.

Secondly, the fact that they couldn't produce the list in a readable format suggests that it isn't in regular use, by banks or anyone. If it were, surely its gnomic qualities would have been brought to the attention of External Relations and – am I being naive? – something would have been done.

Sure enough, when I finally found someone at the Commission who was relatively happy to answer my questions (although she told me not to quote her – another blow against transparency) she told me that there is no mechanism for discovering if anyone is looking at the list.

So, how does the EU make sure that European banks comply with the financial and travel sanctions if they don't keep track of which banks are involving themselves in the programme?

She said that it's the responsibility of individual states to do this, and no state has ever been challenged by the EU about compliance.

I'll just let that sink in for a while … The European Union, which has a long-winded statement about its fundamental values in the preamble for its constitution, has bothered to put together a list of people whom it dislikes strongly enough to ban them from its territories and from banking here. But it doesn't enforce the banking ban.

Still, at least it prevents these murderers, rapists, torturers and oppressors from visiting us. That would be the purpose of the list then?

Well, no. It's hard to forget the image of Robert Mugabe's happy smiling face as he warmly clasped the hand of Prince Charles at Pope John Paul II's funeral in April 2005. He's on the sanctions list, partly because he has knowingly presided over the starvation of millions in Zimbabwe – but he got special dispensation from Italy to travel to the Vatican.

Mugabe has also visited London and Paris within the past five years. So it's hard not to conclude that the list of people and organisations against whom the EU has sanctions is not worth the paper on which it's printed – not that it's often printed out at all.

The EU's 'new' constitution would create the position of Foreign Minister for the European Union. But what would this minister be responsible for? There are 25 different foreign policies within the EU – each of its member states has one – and the chances of getting agreement about what to do on any given problem are minimal. Saddam Hussein's name is also on the list, but – beyond agreeing that he was 'A Bad Man' – when the UN mandated action against him there was no European consensus on what form the action should take. It's one thing to put his name on a list, but another entirely to have an enforceable foreign policy to deal with him.

As with the Balkans in the early 1990s, responsibility for putting words into action against Saddam Hussein in 2003 ultimately fell to the US because its institutions had the clarity to make it possible. It's a superpower in the old-fashioned sense of the word. The existence of the European Union has far-reaching implications for the rest of the world in terms of political, social and economic empire-building. But militarily – and, in fact, in any sense in which words must be translated into force – the EU is not the organisation to look to.

# In 2002 there were two official cases of piracy in European waters – around 1 per cent of the real total

'It was about 1.45 am when I felt that someone had opened my bedroom door', remembered Captain Mayank Mishra. In March 2001, he was commanding the Norwegian-registered *Spar Eight*, a vast hollow mountain of a container ship. After discharging coal for three days at Ghent in Belgium the ship was due, in the morning, to shift to the next berth to load scrap for Turkey.

'They must have sensed my movement because they grabbed my hands and legs and tied me with strong nylon ropes. They were masked and carrying torches. The guy in front of me had a knife in one hand and a watch with a green dial. The one behind me claimed he had a gun pointed at my head. I don't know if that was true.'

'They taped my mouth and asked me to produce the keys to the ship's safe, which I showed them lying nearby. But the safe also had a number lock and, in order to open that, they released one of my hands. In the dark and with my fear that in all probability I would be dead in a few minutes, I couldn't open it immediately. I'd recently joined the vessel and only operated the lock twice.'

'Seeing me fumbling, they threatened to cut off my fingers and then kill me. By this time I had got back some control and tried to explain to them that if they freed my arms I would do a better job. But they didn't take me at my word, kept threatening me and hitting me repeatedly with their torch butt.'

'It was becoming too much for me, as well as for them and they were getting impatient. I pointed towards my trousers, which were hanging up nearby. They had my wallet in them, containing about $400. The men took it and left the cabin, leaving me tied up on the floor. It took me about 40 minutes to untie myself before I could get out and raise the alarm.'

They were gone, back through the ship's warren of corridors

and the thin security veil around the carrier. Since he was in Belgium and not Indonesia or Somalia, where piracy is rampant, Captain Mishra had believed that the risk was low. Europe, he thought – as we all do – is relatively 'safe'. But in the event, the statistics became irrelevant.

Captain Mishra, born and brought up in India, was 31 at the time and, three years on, his attackers haven't been caught. He was badly shaken by the experience and with a baby girl at home he chose not to return to the sea, taking an office job with his firm in Mumbai. He was deeply upset with himself for letting it happen and also with the Belgian authorities, who told him only that there had been two Ghanaians up to similar tricks around the port for some time. How could they be so sure of their nationality, he wondered, since they evidently hadn't caught them?

Modern piracy has little in common with the yo-ho-ho-ing, parrots and big hats we routinely associate with the word. Like 'cybercrime', it carries an aura of glamour that is entirely spurious: the people who commit it have the same basic disregard for other people as any other thief, rapist or murderer.

But the romanticisation of pirates has been made easy since the 17th and 18th centuries. Several colonial powers, including Britain and the United States, handed out licences to 'privateers' to assault the shipping of rival countries in the name of making the seas safe for their own nation's trade, while filling treasury coffers. They stole on behalf of their sponsors, which gave them an edgy legitimacy, but were regarded as pirates by all but the nation who gave them their letter of marque. European powers renounced the practice in 1856 when they signed the Declaration of Paris; the US did so when it signed the Hague conventions of 1899 and 1907. But pirates sail on in the popular imagination.

In fact, as long as there have been boats – which in Europe has been at least since the time of the Phoenicians (12th century BC) – other people have looked at them and their cargoes with a speculative eye. Julius Caesar is supposed to have been held for ransom by pirates in the Mediterranean in about 75 BC.

The sea, with its tempests, triangles and freak waves, is a strange environment for people. Its otherness attracts and repels like waves pulling and sucking. Anything – chirpy cabin boys and pieces of eight included – that humanises it for us has a very deep psychological appeal.

The idea that piracy happens in Europe today, though, is difficult. It implies a lack of law, order and basic safety that is, after all, a very large part of what Europe is supposed to have going for it.

In 2002, there were 383 recorded incidences of piracy worldwide – the vast majority were outside Europe, although they often involved European ships and crews. The Strait of Malacca in the South China Sea is the epicentre of the problem these days, the modern-day equivalent of the 18th-century waters around the island of Hispaniola (now known as Haiti and the Dominican Republic). Hispaniola was where the first pirates' den of retired European privateers sprang up, and was the place that the ship in *Treasure Island* was named after.

The International Maritime Organisation (IMO) has complete records of two or three incidents a year in Europe. But Eric Ellen, a former director of the International Maritime Bureau, was quoted in the *Christian Science Monitor* in 1992 saying that no more than 1 per cent of piracy incidents are actually reported.

Brice Martin-Castex of the IMO explained: 'Our official statistics are what we call a "dark number". Maybe if someone lost his life it is worth reporting it. But if you wish to make a complaint about something that is basically pilfering, it can take two or three days for an investigation and this is valuable time for a commercial shipping operator.' Take into account the loss of business when customers learn that you've been attacked and it's better simply not to report it.

In August 2002, the *Patarhei* yacht simply vanished while moored off the coast of Italy. And in March 2002 eight men boarded the *Blade Runner* (a Maltese bulk carrier) off the coast of Bulgaria, stealing money and valuables from the crew. Both of these incidents are fully reported in the IMO's records.

But many other events received fleeting mentions in the daily maritime newspaper *Lloyd's List* without making it into the official figures – because nobody filed an insurance claim or contacted the police.

Although piracy is real, it's a small risk in comparison with many others at sea, including grounding, technical failure and ocean-inflicted damage.

The financial losses involved are a tiny proportion of the trillions of euros'-worth of goods that are moved across the world's oceans each year. The only certain effect of reporting a boarding by pirates – who carry Uzis rather than cutlasses these days and rarely risk the frippery of a Jolly Roger flag – is to put clients off using your services. Couple this with the delays that lodging reports can cause, and it's often cheaper to pay off the crews and their families regardless of how serious the incident.

So the crime goes largely unreported on commercial shipping and the most serious cost involved is the human cost. It can be terrifying for those involved because of the already dangerous nature of the environment, and when you couple it with the isolation of living on a ship, the experience can be permanently debilitating when it's not actually fatal.

In 1996 a motor yacht called *Carenia* was boarded by four armed pirates while moored in a cove off Corfu. They had pulled alongside in a speedboat and although the yacht owner tried to defend himself with a shotgun, he was overcome and his vessel was boarded and ransacked for valuables. When Greek police arrived, a gun battle took place, the boat owner was killed and the pirates escaped.

Which is not very jolly at all, really.

The risk of piracy in European waters gives the lie to Europe's reputation as a 'safe' place in comparison with the rest of the world. We don't even know for sure just how unsafe our waters really are.

# Every New Year's Eve, millions of Europeans watch a British comedy sketch unknown in Britain

*Dinner for One*, starring Freddie Frinton and May Warden, is a short black-and-white comedy sketch recorded for German television in 1963, which has become a cult tradition on television around the world, especially in northern Europe.

In less than fifteen minutes, it tells the peculiar story of an elderly lady, Miss Sophie, and her butler James, who are enacting a tradition themselves – an anniversary meal with four of Miss Sophie's admirers, all of whom, unfortunately, have died. So the loyal butler plays the part of each of the four men – Sir Toby, Admiral Von Schneider, Mr Pomeroy and Mr Winterbottom – and gives a series of toasts to Miss Sophie's health. Unsurprisingly, since he is drinking for four, he's soon legless.

Weaving around the room like a comedy penguin, he serves Miss Sophie a meal of mulligatawny soup with dry sherry, North Sea haddock with white wine, chicken with champagne, and fruit with port, frequently tripping over the head of a tiger-skin rug.

Before each course James asks: 'Same procedure as last year, Miss Sophie?' – to be told by the amiable old girl: 'Same procedure as every year.' Then, in a faintly surreal twist, she announces that she wishes to retire to bed, indicating that James should lend her a supportive arm. 'Same procedure as last year?' asks the inebriated butler. 'Same procedure as every year', she smiles. 'Well, I'll do my very best', he responds, treating the audience to a big, dirty wink.

A couple of youngish Europeans I know said that it took them years, passing out of childhood, to get the implication of the final wink – and that when they did, it was a shock on a par with realising that Santa Claus doesn't exist.

The bawdy nod to geriatric sex in what looks like an Edwardian setting is part of its cult appeal, though Frinton's physical comedy gets more laughs from the studio audience. He was spotted by the show's producers performing *Dinner for One* at the Winter Gardens

116

in Blackpool, where among his other acts was a comedy drunk, complete with broken cigarette: he had had years to get James's drunkenness right.

It's a fixture on German TV, where it has been shown more than 230 times over 40-odd years, entering the *Guinness Book of Records*. But it also appears as a New Year's treat in Norway, Sweden, Denmark, Greenland, Switzerland (a rival Swiss version also starring Frinton was recorded for the Montreux Festival), Austria, Luxembourg, Estonia, Finland, Holland, Australia and South Africa.

Despite the fact that Frinton died in 1969, aged only 54, he would be delighted to know that his show has gone on to develop an off-screen life of its own. Amateur actors perform stage versions across the continent, often at restaurants serving the meal consumed by Miss Sophie; there's a German band called Admiral Von Schneider; a German woman from the original studio audience, Sonya Guth, is a minor celebrity because her hysterical laughter nearly marred the recording; and a distinct rivalry exists between the German and Swiss versions of the show.

'It was funny', said Nora Harding, Frinton's widow, who lives in Stanmore, north London. 'We had a Swiss television crew come by at Christmas last year and all they were really interested in was getting me to say that the Swiss version was better than the German one, although, to be honest, I wouldn't know the difference.'

When I met Mrs Harding, who had four children with Frinton and remarried after his death, she said that she was anxious to contradict a rumour repeated in a Danish documentary that Frinton had hated the Germans.

She said that although he had been in a wartime entertainment troupe, the story, originally reported by a German journalist, was untrue. 'I don't understand why the young man said that. My husband never hated anyone', she said. 'I remember that when Freddie finally bought himself a nice car he went and bought a BMW. Is that something that he would have done if he hated Germans? I kept it in the driveway for nearly a year after he passed away. I couldn't bring myself to part with it.'

Even a rumour like that couldn't knock a hole in the show's popularity now, though. Its fame has grown since the late 1980s, when the German enthusiasm for Miss Sophie's New Year became infectious – like a particularly soupy cold.

The big curiosity about *Dinner for One*, though, is that it has never been shown on British television: notoriously, it doesn't amuse its originators. By the time I came to watch it myself, I had been warned about this so many times that I was faintly relieved not to find it funny: no freak, me.

Its popularity elsewhere has been analysed at length, though. A German academic suggested that the secret of its success stems from the fact that when people laugh at the farce of Miss Sophie's and James's situation they are really laughing at themselves. After all, he said, the regularity with which New Year comes around makes us all uncomfortably aware that we are trapped in a cycle. 'Same procedure as last year?' we can't avoid asking ourselves, and the answer is best laughed off.

Also, the element of ritual involved in the yearly programming and the dialogue's repetitious nature reportedly have a calming effect on viewers. The Germans have a word – *gemütlich* – to describe something that is homey, comfortable, cosy and genial, and this seems to be very much how European viewers experience *Dinner for One*.

So what is it about the sketch that irritates the British? It must have made us laugh once, since Freddie Frinton was a household name.

Well, firstly there's a sense in which Miss Sophie and James are stereotypes of Englishness that people who know the country only from its old television shows could quite easily imagine. If you take the Major from *Fawlty Towers*, inject him with a near-fatal dose of *Upstairs, Downstairs* and then hit him over the head with the David Lean film version of *Great Expectations* so that tiny icons of Miss Havisham swim around him, you get a rough idea of what *Dinner for One* is like.

On top of the cheesiness, *Dinner for One* demonstrates explicit class issues that you rarely see on the BBC now because they make the British uncomfortable. The deference of James and easy command of Miss Sophie are no longer versions of ourselves that we choose to recognise, although this is apparently how much of the world still sees us.

Master and servant, butler and mistress: when these roles appear on British television these days they usually get the full-blown BBC costume-drama treatment, allowing us to distance ourselves and enjoy the production values, or they are subverted by taking the servants' point of view, as in *Gosford Park*. With its nudge-nudge ending, *Dinner for One* falls uncomfortably between these approaches and is hard for a British audience to take.

There are plenty who despise modern British television and wouldn't watch reality TV unless their lives depended on it. The sketch would certainly be something different, perhaps even exotic, on a Christmas TV schedule, and the fact that it comes with a hinterland could only enhance its creaky appeal.

As it is, *Dinner for One*'s absence from TV screens in its country of origin represents a failure by the British to laugh at themselves – an accusation that we regularly and gaily throw at others. 'Same procedure as last year?' is to the Germans what 'Don't mention the war' in *Fawlty Towers* is to the British. Perhaps we could organise some kind of cultural hostage exchange?

# If state pension schemes were judged in the same way as the private sector, many European treasury ministers would be in prison

In 1903, an enterprising Italian scoundrel called Charles Ponzi immigrated to the United States and promptly got jailed for forging cheques. Yet within twenty years he became one of Boston's best-known millionaires, having also made many other people rather wealthy in the process.

His get-rich-quick scheme was based on a lie: if people gave him their money he would invest it in international postal coupons, speculate on the devaluation of international currencies and double their money in 90 days.

It seemed to work: the money-doubling part, at least. For eight months or so he accepted increasingly large amounts of cash from investors who had heard of the scheme from satisfied customers. At one point he was taking more than a million a week.

The rub, though, was that he was not investing the money in anything. He was simply taking the cash from new investors to pay the dividends of the earlier ones. It worked because many investors decided to plough their dividends back in the same place – nowhere else produced comparable returns – putting off the moment when the whole pyramid would collapse.

When it did, Mr Ponzi ended up back in prison, feted by the people he had made rich, loathed by those whose money he had lost, but widely admired for his chutzpah.

Most European state pensions work on exactly the same principle, with the distinction that today's retirees are the fortunate investors and their children are the losers. There are no national insurance savings quietly earning interest in the background, no pension nest eggs waiting to hatch. The market is not weaving any magic for the young taxpayer or providing a dividend for careful government investments. It's simply as if there were a tube sucking cash from the pockets of grey-faced young workers and depositing it in the wallets of their retired parents. Today's government pensions are paid from the national insurance of today's working young.

Next time you see a Saga advertisement for a world cruise featuring beaming, bronzed baby boomers tossing their platinum locks, bear in mind that – unless you are there already – their delight is largely at your expense. There are forces at work ensuring that this generation of retirees are the wealthiest ever and that this won't be repeated.

The pay-as-you-go pension system was invented, like Germany, by Otto von Bismarck and in 1889 it worked well. This was because the active workforce vastly outnumbered the retired population, for the simple reason that the retirement age was 70 and the average life expectancy only 48.

But life expectancy has been on the rise for the past 300 years. It shot up particularly quickly in the second half of the 20th century and continues to increase.

Postwar prosperity brought along with it the baby-boomers, whose parents' memories of wartime deprivation and (perhaps resulting) generosity to their children helped to create the first generation that was selfish and proud of it: teenagers. They had rock'n'roll, peace and love, contraception, foreign holidays, silly haircuts or no haircuts at all. They were talkin' 'bout their generation and had a hard job empathising with any other because their material circumstances were so unique. Still are.

In Britain they received unprecedented educational opportunities – grammar schools, technical colleges and grants to go to university – which created enviable social mobility. But they subsequently abolished this mobility when they achieved political power, in an old-fashioned manoeuvre known as 'pulling up the ladder'. Across Europe, this generation didn't have large families – which would have compromised the standard of living made possible for them by their parents – and so they created a demographic time-bomb that will detonate when their children hope to retire in 30 or so years' time.

Between 1960 and 1965 the overall birth rate in the European Union was 2.7 children per woman, which was comfortably above the rate of 2.1 needed to maintain the size of the population (one to replace each parent and the 'point one' to compensate for fatal mishaps). By 2005 it had fallen to 1.5 children per woman. In Italy and Spain, which have the lowest birth rates in the world, it was only 1.3.

At the same time the average European is living longer so that with every passing year the pensions problem gets worse: there are fewer young people paying for more older people. Politicians have realised that the issue is a poison chalice and have passed responsibility for pensions to the private sector and the individual instead. Unfortunately one of the knock-on effects of this is that many companies are less likely to employ permanent staff, since this usually means pension contributions. This also means that it's harder for young people than it was for their parents to get jobs, as opposed to freelance or contract work.

In turn this makes it less likely that they will be able to achieve the stability necessary to start a family – a job with a steady income and a home. This generation will probably also have only a small number of children, but as a result of being unable to afford more, or of having to delay a family until just before menopause, rather than any more cheerful kind of a choice. Also, without a full-time job it's hard to maintain a private pension.

What you have coming up now is a generation of working young who received nothing from the state, except an often-shoddy education to secondary level, and were then charged for the university degree that their parents' generation got for free. Equally, they can expect nothing of any value in the future, since there will be no pensions to speak of, and it's a matter for speculation whether state healthcare will survive the tsunami of demand that will be placed upon it by long-lived retirees. Today's young Europeans have been dealt a rotten hand. It's a form of disenfranchisement. In later life, many young people will discover that they can't even live in their parents' comfortable homes – the threshold for inheritance tax is set too low relative to the cost of the property, and they will have to sell the houses to pay it. When this happens, it seems likely that all hell will break loose, politically speaking.

There's a poem that springs to mind called 'When I am an old woman I shall wear purple', by a British poet called Jenny Joseph.

Born in 1932, she is probably considering breaking out her violet accessories by now. It describes a retiree living the life of Riley, carefree in her irresponsibility. 'I shall spend my pension on brandy and summer gloves and satin sandals and say we've no money for butter', it runs, painting a delightful picture of a colourful old lady with nothing better to do than run umbrellas noisily along railings and eat her way through loaves of bread and pickle ... Yet 'Pension? What pension?' is the question that the generation following Ms Joseph will ask. This question is even more pertinent for women, since breaks from work to have children will only compound their financial woes. They will probably work into their seventies and, saddest of all, will have to forget about satin sandals entirely.

So is there a glimmer of hope? Perhaps. But first a false dawn. Immigration is often brandished as a good liberal solution to the problems of falling birth rates. Yet unfortunately the truth is that no sooner does a young couple arrive from Bangladesh, for example, to contribute to the economy and start a family, than the realisation dawns on them – the way to afford the things that they would like is to have fewer children than they would in Bangladesh. The birth rate drops within two generations to the European level: after all, if they wanted a lower standard of living they could have stayed put.

So how to withstand the relentless onslaught of grey power? Well, two things spring to mind. Firstly, the young working population needs to get politically organised in the same way as their parents. If they don't do it soon it may be too late: the various governments of Europe will vacuum up the inheritance tax and spend it on tax breaks for retired rich voters (who will spend it on holidays), while simultaneously declaring that all these new-fangled advances in treatment for the elderly have put the health systems out of business for anything except broken limbs and migraines.

And secondly: young people of Europe, have as many children as you can afford! And by this I don't include the cost of buying each of them luxury items like mobile telephones and DVD players. Comfort yourself (if not them) with the thought that only adults really appreciate these things anyway, because we have lived in a world without them. Take a leaf out of your own parents' book and see the kids as a financial proposition. But this time let's think about the long term.

## DID DAVID HASSELHOFF END THE COLD WAR?

More children would mean more financial security for everyone. Not only will there be more of them to pay for our pensions, but some of them might even end up being fond of us and take care of us in our dotage. It would be safety in numbers.

# In the former Soviet bloc, more women than men request sex changes – the opposite to the rest of the world

In the Czech Republic and Slovakia there are three times as many female-to-male transsexuals as male to female, according to the Institute of Sexology at the Charles University in Prague. Similarly, the *International Encyclopaedia of Sexuality* says that in the Ukraine there are many more women wanting to become men than in western Europe – where the usual ratio is three or four men to one woman. Stunningly, in Poland there are seven women asking for the surgery for each man in a similar position.

In the West, sex-change operations are often documented in a titillating way, from the point of view of the people most directly involved. The most common narrative is that they were uncomfortable in their skin right from the start, and it's presented as a black-and-white issue. There are all kinds of biological and chemical factors put forward as explanations for individual cases, yet when one turns to Eastern Europe, one sees that something different is going on.

'The statistics available from Eastern Europe are very interesting', said Dr Russell Reid, a consultant psychiatrist specialising in sex-change candidates at Hillingdon Hospital in London. 'Because they show that there is a cultural aspect to wanting to change your sex.'

Under otherwise normal circumstances, deciding to change one of the most basic things about oneself – one's sex – must involve an unusual degree of focus on the 'problem', as well as a certain amount of egocentricity. Dr Russell explained that there's a large grey area between feeling uncomfortable with oneself and deciding that the solution would be to have a sex-change operation.

Yet gender dysphoria is a psychological condition with which people had to cope until the 20th century. And it's into this grey area that the 'extra' women from the former Soviet bloc who wish to become men apparently fall.

Life for women in Russia and Eastern Europe through the last century was notoriously hard. After the Russian revolution in 1917, the Bolsheviks declared that women had been 'liberated' – but this swiftly came to mean that being unemployed was an imprisonable offence for women as well as for men. Child-rearing wasn't regarded as work, and in addition to the 'double burden' that women all over the world frequently carry, Soviet citizens were also expected to find the time to attend political meetings.

Soviet author Natalia Baranskaia wrote a book called *A Week Like Any Other* in the 1960s. Although 'fiction', it details the life of a Soviet mother attempting to hold down her job as a research scientist while running a house, a child, a husband and attending to all the other duties and problems that living under the Soviet regime involved. It's a hard but compelling read that makes Allison Pearson's *I Don't Know How She Does It* – which covers similar ground but is set in modern Britain – seem like the whining of an over-privileged brat by comparison. The element of state coercion makes all the difference.

One of the most noticeable features of the Soviet novel is the absence of any commentary on the central character's life. The reality, as well as the fiction, was that Soviet women made no complaints because they had been 'liberated' and to suggest otherwise was a political crime. The author had to allow the facts to speak for themselves and keep her fingers crossed.

'The problem with the "liberation" of Russian women was that it was done by men', said Dr Margot Light of the London School of Economics' International Studies department. 'I remember going there in the 1960s and being amazed, as we crossed the border, that the navvies by the side of the railway were women. The economy was geared towards heavy industry and women were both the means of production and reproduction.'

'But life was made extremely hard by the fact that the consumerism side of the economy was neglected. All the products that made life easier in the West for mothers – washing machines, sanitary materials, baby food, contraception – just didn't exist. When I went, I took an entire suitcase full of tampons because they didn't have them … I was going for quite a while.'

The Soviet regime didn't value 'feminine' qualities because they couldn't be used to produce steel plates or dig coal. The ideal, as shown in state artwork, involved women with big, meaty forearms and broad shoulders toiling in the fields and factories alongside their men.

It played havoc with relationships between men and women by removing the defining autonomy of being the sole provider that traditionally characterises male behaviour and instead imposing a set of state targets. What happened was a mass male descent into alcoholism and a flight from their families, where they felt they had no role. A mere fifteen years after the end of the Soviet era, Russian divorce statistics still show no sign of improving, and put western Europe in the shade.

Abortion was the only available means of contraception – although there was a period between 1936 and 1955 during which it was illegal. The entry of women into the workplace had slowed up the growth of the population – or 'workforce' – and making the only available form of contraception illegal was intended to address this problem. If this was women's liberation, it was fundamentally different to the kind that Western women hoped for.

Once at work, women were paid less than men for doing the same job, or found that professions that they came to dominate, including medicine, became less prestigious as a result. Does this sound familiar?

In Poland, the sexual inequities were compounded by the Catholic Church. The Church's older set of norms for the behaviour of women never really disappeared, despite Soviet attempts to impose atheism on the country. So added to the uncertainty about whether one's womanhood was valued, and on what terms, there were also strictures about not behaving like Mary Magdalene – whoever she was. No wonder Poland's women remain to this day more confused about their gender identity than anyone else in the world (as evidenced by the sex-change statistics) – cultural attitudes take decades to change.

It's possible that there are also more lesbian women in countries under former Soviet rule who want to become men. Soviet authorities saw homosexuality as a serious crime. While lesbianism was never regarded as dangerous in the same way as male homosexuality, lesbian women in Eastern bloc countries could well have adopted these subconscious attitudes. For those wanting a sex-change, part of their thought process may be: 'I want to have sex with women. Only men have sex with women. I'm really a man.'

There's a grey area between those who are a little unsure of their gender identity and those who ultimately ask for surgery. But when it comes to explaining why there's such disparity in the numbers of women asking for sex changes in the former Soviet bloc compared to the rest of the world, what else could it be but the inequities of day-to-day life?

As Dr Reid suggested: 'It is possible that life for women in that part of the world was – and is – so grim that they just want to be men.'

# Forty per cent of homes in Romania don't have running water

Romania may be joining the European Union on 1 January 2007 or thereafter. In 2002 the *Economist* magazine ranked its standard of living between that of Libya and Lebanon and its per capita Gross Domestic Product about on a par with Namibia and Paraguay. It's a pretty good example of how and why the EU expands.

In 1993, at a summit in Copenhagen, the EU invited applications for membership from former Soviet bloc countries. Why? Broadly its long-term interests lie in expansion, because the larger it is, the more seriously it will be taken and the more powerful it will be. When it comes to empire, bigger is always better.

By drawing in countries on its borders, the EU defends itself against the usual things (envious neighbours, belligerent totalitarian regimes, poverty and its results) and also remakes the world in its own image.

The EU's strategy could be seen as colonialism turned on its head: a form of domination in which new members are clamouring to be let in. Or perhaps its expansion should be viewed as a political experiment to challenge a more old-fashioned but still popular model, in which a country (Afghanistan, Iraq) gets invaded and its regime changed, leaving behind varying degrees of chaos in the name of self-determination.

Applications to join the EU are judged by the 1993 'Copenhagen criteria'. The summit agreed:

> Membership requires that the candidate country has achieved stability of institutions guaranteeing democracy, the rule of law, human rights and respect for and protection of minorities, the existence of a functioning market economy, as well as the capacity to cope with competitive pressure and market forces within the Union. Membership presupposes the candidate's ability to take on the obligations of membership, including adherence to the aims of political, economic and monetary union.

In other words, if you want to join our club, you've got to be more like us.

The process is a long one for Romania. It's had trouble meeting the Copenhagen criteria because of its treatment of the Roma minority and political corruption. But there's serious money being spent on the place by the taxpayers of western Europe.

Millions are given to Romania for specific purposes, like improving the water supply. The Romanian government carries out improvements, while the EU monitors proceedings. A clearer example of the carrot-and-stick approach is hard to imagine: the EU gives large amounts of cash to Romania, tells them to sort out their problems and then berates them publicly when they fail to get it right. If things go wrong the EU has the power to make them wait longer to join.

There are three major programmes helping Romania achieve its goal of EU membership. These include Poland–Hungary Actions for Economic Reconstruction (PHARE) and the Special Accession Programme for Agriculture and Rural Development (SAPARD). The third, the Instrument for Structural Policies for Pre-Accession (ISPA), provides help with transport and environment infrastructure – so homes with no running water fall squarely under this programme.

A 2002 EU report said: 'Romania faces acute problems concerning air, water and soil pollution – all of which require large-scale investments from both the public and the private sectors. The major environmental impact is the poor quality of water, which results from the discharge of untreated or partially treated waste water.' Homes without taps are the least of its problems.

'The population without running water is mainly in villages and rural areas. They have access to wells', said Cesar Niculescu, an engineer working for the EU in Romania. 'There is no specific measure in ISPA saying that the whole population must have centralised drinking water, taps in their homes. What it says is that they should have access to drinking water of a certain quality.'

'So the quality of water from the village wells is an issue. Most are not dug very deep and the underground water is polluted with chemicals from the soil.'

'In these rural areas they don't have a centralised system for sewage or waste water. In most cases what exists is a "septic tank". But generally these are not real tanks – just a hole in the ground where waste is put. It is very easy for this water to pollute the water table.'

Basically, these EU programmes speed up the process of 'modernisation' that took decades, if not hundreds of years in western Europe. There are pockets of relative poverty in every EU country, but the billions being spent in Romania is redistribution of wealth on an international scale. And what could be more important than clean water to a modern European standard of living? The principle of water-borne disease was established during the 19th century, so how could a country whose entry to the EU is under consideration remain subject to the spectres of cholera and typhoid?

Yet what is being done in Romania leading up to the proposed joining date in 2007 is only the basics. The Copenhagen criteria state that a functioning market economy and a firm grasp of the fundamentals of democracy have to be in place in order to join the EU. But in the meantime, the EU is also laying the groundwork for Romania to become the newest part of the huge market for goods and services.

'It all comes down to money and business', said Martyn Birchill, who works for a consortium of British water companies in Romania that won EU contracts to improve infrastructure. 'The 40 per cent of the population who don't have mains water are not paying for their water at all, because it is not metered.'

'We don't have any plans to take mains water to areas that don't already have it – although we are part of a long-term project that may see it happen eventually. We are improving the existing infrastructure so that mains pipes don't leak and the wells are dug to a proper depth and can be metered,' he said.

What the EU is trying to do is put things on a better financial footing so that Romania will be in a position to buy services from the private sector. It would be no good proposing that companies should provide clean water that Romanians can't pay for, because it's unknown how much water a given household or business uses.

Bad infrastructure affects Romania's ability to be a functioning market economy because, for instance, without knowing how much water a factory uses and charging appropriately, one factory may receive an unfairly large bill, putting it at a competitive disadvantage. And what is true on a factory-by-factory basis is also true on a national level. Without decent infrastructure the place won't be attractive to investors.

One of Mr Birchill's observations was that Romania's water infrastructure today is similar to that in parts of Britain in the 1950s and 1960s. This has profound implications.

Without running water in homes, it isn't possible to plumb in washing machines, meaning that women spend hours playing the role of 'washing machine' themselves. While this is the case, it's difficult for them to extricate themselves from domestic servitude and work outside the house.

The EU's constitution, title 3, article II-83 says: 'Equality between men and women must be ensured in all areas, including employment, work and pay.' But without running water to clean the family's clothes and bed linen, how could you physically make it to the workplace – not to mention the hours you'd spend collecting water, then boiling or heating it for drinking, cooking and bathing? Running water is a prerequisite for many of the consumer advances that have made the lifestyle of today's west European women possible.

Whether Romania joins the EU in 2007 or not, it will be a long time before life there becomes similar to life in western Europe.

# There was an island in the Azores called Sabrina that vanished

*There's a schooner in the offing*
*With her top sails shot with fire*
*And my heart has gone aboard her*
*For the islands of desire*
     from 'The Sea Gypsy' by Richard Hovey

History doesn't record Captain Tillard's first name: for the most part he is simply Captain Tillard of the British sloop-of-war, *Sabrina*. Yet you can picture the scene ... In 1811, he stumbled upon an island in the Atlantic Ocean that was unmarked on any of his charts. Perhaps oddly, it appeared to be steaming and nothing much was growing on it. Nonetheless, he and a small party of officers – in their navy blue outfits, white stockings and gold epaulettes – clambered ashore, struggled to the island's highest point and planted a Union Jack like the obedient little empire-builders that they were. Having claimed it as Great Britain's newest territory and named it after their ship, they sailed away – probably taking pride in a job well done.

Strangely, though, when the Admiralty's survey ship passed that way four months later to nail Sabrina's coordinates and particulars, the island had completely vanished. There was nothing left behind but a pungent whiff of ... what was that? Fantasy? Bullshit? Madness?

In fact, it was probably some kind of sulphurous gas – all of the Azorean islands are volcanic in origin, and the short-lived island of Sabrina, found a mile off the coast of St Michael (or San Miguel as it's known now), was no exception.

At its largest, Sabrina was about 330 feet above sea level and one mile long. But, physical reality aside, as a metaphor for the pointlessness of sticking flags in things, this story is hard to beat.

## DID DAVID HASSELHOFF END THE COLD WAR?

'You can't take it with you' – so you could be forgiven for finding it amusing that something as apparently solid as an island beat the British Empire to it and decolonised itself in the most final way imaginable.

The Azores are now Portuguese islands spread over 373 miles of the North Atlantic, two hours' flying time from their administrative capital, Lisbon, and five from the east coast of the United States. Today, 243,000 people live on the nine islands that make up the archipelago.

The land is formed from the upper sections of volcanoes, which have underwater origins resulting from three tectonic plates meeting in a T-shaped junction. The North American, African and Eurasian plates are pulling apart on the seabed and the gaps between them are filled by molten material that forms a new oceanic crust, in a process that continues today.

As I write, there's a submarine eruption taking place six miles west of the island of Terceira in an area called Serreta High. This sally from the insides of the Earth began in 1998 and the superficial evidence for it is plumes of smoke coming from lava debris. Basalt magma spews from the ocean floor with gas trapped inside it, creating balloons that float upwards and making the area dangerous for shipping.

The sudden arrival – and disappearance – of Sabrina was documented by the German naturalist Baron Alexander von Humboldt (1768–1859) in his five-volume *Kosmos*. But there's a much fuller description in *North Atlantic Memoir* by Alexander George Findlay, published in 1873 and still available in the library of the National Maritime Museum at Greenwich, London. Judging by his introduction, Findlay drew on the resources of the British government's hydrographical department and the accounts provided by British naval officers who were in the area at the time, including good old Captain Tillard. This was only six years after the Battle of Trafalgar and there's a strong possibility that some of the sailors who provided the information may also have been involved in that pivotal moment of European history.

*North Atlantic Memoir* says that from the early part of 1811, 'innumerable quantities of fish, some nearly roasted, and others as if broiled, floated on the surface of the sea towards the shore' of St Michael. Flames were first seen above the surface of the water on 1 February and a ship – the brig *Swift* – was lost with her entire crew on this spot before the existence of the hazard beneath the surface was well known.

Then on 18 June that year, the mouth of the volcano's crater showed itself above water for the first time. 'The smoke drew up several waterspouts which, spreading in the air, fell in heavy rain, accompanied with vast quantities of black sand that completely covered the *Sabrina*'s deck, at the distance of three or four miles,' Findlay wrote. It must have been an astonishing thing to witness – with conditions that turned day into night, producing a visual representation of doomsday for the superstitious sailor.

Then, on 4 July, *North Atlantic Memoir* records that 'a complete island was formed and perfectly quiet'. From a high cliff on nearby St Michael, 'the first appearance was that of an immense body of smoke revolving in the water, when suddenly would shoot up a column of the blackest cinders, ashes and stones in form like a spire ... These bursts were accompanied by explosions of the most vivid lightning, with the noise like the continual firing of canon and musketry.'

Yet by the middle of October 1811, no part of Sabrina was left above the water, having been washed away by the waves, and only a dangerous sub-surface accumulation of magma remained – although by now its existence was at least well known. In 1812, smoke was again seen issuing from the spot, but by 1841 a Captain Vidal (they never have first names) anchored HMS *Styx* there, and recorded at least 15 fathoms of water.

There are around 200 islands mentioned on 19th-century nautical charts and atlases that are now known not to exist: they are the imaginary 'islands of desire' of Richard Hovey's poem, conjured into being by the people who needed them. The oldest are often real islands, whose positions were poorly determined due to the difficulties involved in calculating longitude until the 18th century, and then given a lease of life by a lazy time-lag in correcting the maps. They arose because the urgencies of trade and empire put a premium on cartography even before the tools existed to guarantee accuracy.

Others of these islands were the result of errors in reporting, charting and typography. Some may have been born of fraud – discovering and naming an island after oneself might well appeal to the starved ego of an islomane cast adrift at sea for too long, or might add credence to a rascal seeking financial backing for an imaginary voyage. Others still may have been optical illusions: low cloud banks glimpsed on a horizon in unusual weather conditions.

Publishing legend has it that atlases also sometimes contain deliberate inaccuracies – fantasy islands inserted so that copyright owners can tell if their expensively assembled maps are being ripped off by competitors. If it were true, this practice would be morally questionable, since for a ship in trouble it could mean the difference between life and death.

The real, vanishing island of Sabrina is, among other things, a cautionary tale for the unwary. She rose, appeared solid, made it on to a map and then melted away again, leaving us to ponder that if one can't even be sure of the ground beneath one's feet, then of what can one ultimately be sure? Not all dry land is as dry as it should be, apparently. And if we can't trust the charts by which we navigate, on what basis do we navigate at all?

Plato was responsible for one of the most enduring tall tales of the sea. In the 4th century BC he wrote two books – *Timaeus* and *Critias* – purporting to tell the story of the lost island of Atlantis, a place that he said had flourished 12,000 years previously and then sunk beneath the waves in a day and a night.

Its armies, he said, had conquered large parts of Africa and Europe before being defeated by the Ancient Greeks. He placed it in the Straits of Gibraltar and was working on a third book on the subject when he died. He claimed that his sources were hearsay, word-of-mouth already thousands of years old when it was passed to him: he almost certainly made it up. It's more than likely that he intended it as a parable about the possible fate of Ancient Greece if its people became corrupt and greedy, as the people of Atlantis had done. Poignantly, his myth has outlived the civilisation that it was intended to inform.

In 1882, a United States congressman called Ignatius Donnelly rekindled interest in Atlantis by writing a book called *Atlantis: the*

*Antediluvian World*, which became a bestseller. He located Atlantis in the Azores, where vanishing islands are not entirely unheard of. Ironic, then, that it's better known to this day than Sabrina, which really sank beneath the waves.

# Ukraine is the cradle of European democracy

Ukraine seems to have a border with every other state for hundreds of miles in any direction. Russia, Belarus, Poland, Slovakia, Hungary, Romania, Moldova, the Black Sea and the Sea of Azov form a ring around it. Kiev is the capital, the Carpathian Mountains in the south-west are redolent of Bram Stoker, and Chernobyl sits, glowing, up in the north near the border with Belarus.

It has been politically appropriated by several of its neighbours over the years. Most of Ukraine was incorporated into Poland in 1569, the Ukrainian Cossacks were defeated by Peter I of Russia in 1709 and when Poland was partitioned in 1772, western Ukraine became part of the Austro-Hungarian Empire.

But the country's Cossack identity was strong, preventing it from being washed away by the tides of European history, and herein lies Ukraine's claim to a democratic heritage.

The Cossacks are identified with the steppe, the vast prairie that cuts a swathe across northern Europe – and which is possibly the dullest place on Earth to photograph. Nothing much appears to grow there and it is almost impossibly flat, so it was an ideal environment for people who wanted to make a living by raiding other people's farms. They could sweep across it on horseback every once in a while, and then vanish back into the tundra, leaving a pullulating fear of the unknown in their wake.

The Cossacks were free from the empires competing for the rest of the Ukraine because, initially at least, they lived in a place that nobody else wanted. And the value that they placed on their freedom was high.

In 1709, despite an alliance with Charles XII of Sweden, the Cossacks were overwhelmed by Russian forces and their leader – or *hetman* – was killed. A party of exiles including their new *hetman*, Pylyp Orlyk, rode off to Moldova, where they wrote something that has come to be known as the 'Bendery Constitution', after the town in which it was conceived.

This document was a written constitution for the Cossack nation – nearly eight decades before the American and French revolutions, and their resulting written constitutions – and it's a big deal because conventional histories of practical democracy overlook it.

In the Enlightenment tradition, the Bendery Constitution put limits on the powers of the *hetman*, who had to be elected to his position. As checks against tyranny, he had to agree to a list of sixteen articles circumscribing his actions and guaranteeing the rights and privileges of his officer corps.

The Constitution made provision for regular meetings of a governing body to advise the leader. The *hetman* couldn't initiate emergency action without consulting his committee. Perhaps most importantly, the committee was given the right and duty to criticise their leader.

OK, the document was also written in convoluted Latin and contained derogatory remarks about Jews and Poles. But it was signed by Hetman Orlyk in April 1710 and approved by Charles XII of Sweden. It was Europe's first written constitution, although it was never implemented.

But, you may well ask, what good is this? What's the significance of a document advocating a primitive democracy that was never put to any practical use?

The point is that this document didn't spring up spontaneously. Cossack democracy was not conjured from thin air – how could it be when the constitution involved a significant dispersal of power away from its possessor? A gesture so apparently altruistic implies a strong set of democratic values held by a large group of people: some to be in power and others to hold them to account – a culture of democracy.

Democracy is a habit of mind more than anything else. You can have all the written constitutions and democratic institutions in the world, but without a population who actively understand and uphold democratic values and care passionately when these are infringed, democracy will eventually crumble away ... as it has in Zimbabwe.

So what are the Ukrainian Cossacks' democratic credentials? Their history is very unusual in the sense that Cossack women expect and receive the same degree of freedom that their men enjoy. As long ago as the 9th century, the princesses of Kiev were educated like their brothers. Some might consider it ironic that it was the learned Queen Olga (946–66) who began the country's (very late) conversion to Christianity. Perhaps because Ukraine's encounter with the misogyny of the medieval Church was so late, paganism and Christianity co-existed there for many centuries – and maybe they still do, in a country where the habit of matriarchy was never completely overwhelmed.

In many parts of Ukraine, it was the woman who chose her husband, educated the children and organised the community. Warfare was something with which the men were more involved. But in Ukrainian folklore, it's hard to find examples of women being abused by their spouses or even of marital inequality: the roles of men and women were very similar.

Paul d'Aleppo, an Arabian scholar who travelled in the Ukraine from 1652–3, praised the women he met, saying: 'Whilst almost everywhere else at this epoch women are considered as inferior beings, Ukrainian women were treated as equals with men and were as learned as they.'

In the 17th and 18th centuries, at a time when Mary Wollstonecraft was feeling her way towards the first feminist tract in English, *A Vindication of the Rights of Woman*, Cossack women already had material and moral independence. The money they took into a marriage was theirs, as were inheritances, and the law guaranteed them part of their husband's fortune in the event of widowhood. A Cossack woman had to be consulted about the sale or purchase of any property by her husband and often she was the one in charge of household finances.

A strong tradition of organisations exclusively for women existed in the Ukraine, perhaps as a bulwark against the disappearance of their men across the steppe to war – and this tradition continues today. Even when they found themselves in Nazi refugee camps, Cossack women organised themselves into committees. Once the war was over, these were amalgamated to become the Organisation of Ukrainian Women in Foreign Lands, under the presidency of Irene Pavlykovska.

In fact, wherever Ukrainian women go, they get organised. During the 1960s, while the Ukraine was part of the Soviet Empire, the Association of Ukrainian Women in Great Britain pointed out that 'had Ukraine not lost her independence, the Ukrainian women

would not have had such a long and bitter fight for their own emancipation'.

And this points to a greater truth. Becoming the Soviet Republic
of Ukraine in 1922 set the position of women in that country back
by centuries. Stalin sent many of the leading figures in the women's
movement to Siberia, notwithstanding the fact that the Bolshevik
revolution in 1917 had 'announced' female emancipation. The
Soviets simply made it a point to remove any social obstacle that
stood between the soul of a person and the state.

In this respect, the plight of women in the Ukraine has mirrored
the plight of the entire country. They are freedom-loving, self-
confident and unusually egalitarian, but frequently pushed around
by the Russians.

In 2004, the Ukraine's 'Orange Revolution' finally shook off
the governmental legacy of the Soviet era. But the *International
Encyclopaedia of Sexuality* reports that the psychological violence
done to relations between men and women by Communism will
take decades to repair. 'Lack of autonomy, self-sufficiency, pursuit
of self-interest and competence contributed very much toward the
demasculinization of the male population of Ukraine', wrote Tamara
Govurun and Borys Vornyk, who also describe the resulting Soviet-
style rates of divorce and male alcoholism. Their analysis went on
to suggest how a culture can change over time: 'In a society where
there was a lack of responsibility and respect for personality,
both genders were losing such human characteristics as being
co-operative, warm, sympathetic, loving, creative, and altruistic in
relationships, sensitive to others, and intelligent in communications.'

Yet fascinatingly, Ukraine's 2004 election immediately produced
a female Prime Minister – Yulia Tymoshenko – who is beautiful by
any standards, let alone among politicians: surely it takes a nation
of self-confident men to put a truly beautiful woman in charge? It's
hard to imagine it happening in Britain.

Equality between the sexes is the most fundamental equality,
because opportunities to play out one's true feelings on the matter
arise more frequently for most people than any other prejudice.
And although equality is not all there is to democracy, it's a large
part of it.

## DID DAVID HASSELHOFF END THE COLD WAR?

Based on its past, liberal democracy in the Ukraine would appear to have a real future. All national identities are in some sense built (rather than innate), and after Ukraine's recent upheavals it's only fair to expect that its new identity is still partly under construction. But what great foundations.

# The euro is at least the fifth European single currency

A single European currency is not a new idea and the euro is not the first pan-European currency. For millennia Europeans have been buying and selling: goods needed to be paid for, and where there was a need, a currency emerged.

Coins are unearthed today that are a reminder of a particularly successful international financial and political union that stretched right across Europe, Africa and the Middle East: the Roman Empire. It had a system of gold, silver, bronze and copper coinage with names familiar to anyone who did Latin at school (*denarii*, *sestertii*, etc.). This single currency made the reputation of the Roman Empire concrete for people living in its far-flung regions, and its scope, geographically at least, went far beyond that of the euro today. It was Julius Caesar whose head first appeared on a coin, which was a manipulation that made people think of money as symbolic of politics for the first time.

More recently, in 1830, Belgium adopted the French franc as its medium for exchange, followed by Italy in 1861, Switzerland in 1865, and Greece and Bulgaria in 1867. At the height of its influence, this Latin Monetary Union extended unofficially to eighteen countries, but was eventually destroyed by the First World War.

There was also a Scandinavian monetary union, started by Sweden and Denmark in 1873 and joined by Norway in 1875. They accepted each other's gold coins, bank notes and tokens, measured in krona, and this also lasted until after the First World War.

A third such arrangement, the Zollverein customs union, was made up of lots of tiny local currencies, and was attached to the central bank of Prussia in 1838. In 1856 Austria became associated with it, but it all came to a sticky end in 1866 when Prussia and Austria declared war on each other. Are you beginning to see a pattern emerge?

Five years later, though, in 1871, Germany was born from a tapestry of competing jurisdictions. The Reichsbank was founded four years after that, and the Reichsmark became the legal and

143

only tender of the German Reich. This unit of exchange survived two world wars and devastating inflation in 1923, and lived on until 1999 as the Deutschmark. That year the strength of the German economy and therefore the Deutschmark, coupled with fear of what a re-united Germany might become capable of, brought the euro into being.

'The only one of the twelve countries involved not to benefit from the creation of the euro in economic terms was Germany', said Katinka Barysch, the chief economist at the Centre for European Reform. 'It was created for political reasons related to the reunification of East and West Germany. Europeans remember the Second World War extremely vividly and agreeing to join the euro was Germany's way of saying: "We are good Europeans. You can trust us."' It is also often said that France wouldn't have agreed to German reunification if had not received the euro as a quid pro quo.

For France and the ten other countries involved at the outset, the benefits of being in an official currency union with Germany included finally having a say in what took place at the heart of their own financial affairs. Previously, the Deutschmark's dominance meant that Europe's smaller currencies were exposed to its strength or weakness, without their governments having an effective voice at the Bundesbank.

The single European currency also brought an end to currency speculation in the eurozone, a destabilising force on any economy – for instance, the currency speculation of George Soros is credited with sending Britain crashing out of the eurozone on Black Wednesday.

The euro also boosted trade at a time when German reunification and the expensive problems that it had revealed had cast an economic gloom over Europe. 'But it won't fix economic problems with individual economies. It wasn't supposed to do that. It was basically supposed to eliminate exchange rate risk', said Ms Barysch.

Her think tank's position is to be positive about Europe wherever possible, but constructively critical. While having no animosity towards the idea of joining the euro, she believes that Britain could stay within the European Union but outside the single currency for a very long time. This is because the political cost – having no voice at the European Central Bank in Frankfurt – is one that Britain is prepared to pay.

The City of London, which remains the largest money market in Europe, makes its money partly from currency exchange trans-actions, which were the very thing that the euro was designed to eliminate. So it is inevitable that the British people will hear com-peting views about whether joining the euro would be good for its economy. Even if every academic economist in the country were in favour of joining the euro there would be naysayers from financial institutions in the City, whose profits rely on currency exchange. Both would get plenty of airtime.

But consider this. Britain has a giddying history of rocketing and plunging interest rates. Traditionally, our politicians have manipu-lated the economy for their own purposes – making us richer or poorer according to pending elections, or, worse, simply because of their incompetence.

In 1997, Gordon Brown, the British Chancellor of the Exchequer, handed control of interest rates to the Bank of England, taking politicians out of the equation. He effectively adopted the same model that supported economic prosperity in Germany for dec-ades, and one which the British had a hand in creating after the last war.

If Britain joined the eurozone, it would be agreeing to the same model on a much larger scale.

One of the most important questions is: should we trust the European Central Bank in the same way that we have recently learned to trust the Bank of England? After that, it's largely a question of having the national self-confidence to cope with the economic 'weather' to which we would be exposed. Would our businesses be competitive enough to survive in such a large market? Would the market be sufficiently buoyant in the medium-to long-term to sustain the levels of business that would justify such a short-term upheaval?

Meanwhile the strength of the pound over a long period, while boosting national self-esteem, has also undermined our ability to manufacture things that other countries can afford to buy.

Every currency in the world is used across regions where

economic micro-climates swirl and compete. In Britain the regional variations in house prices testify to varying levels of economic activity throughout the country. It's exactly the same across Europe and the rest of the world, and always has been. Because of this, a single exchange rate sliding up and down will never fit each national economy perfectly at the same time. But what it may do is help to create an economic prosperity that could compensate for this by opening up larger markets, particularly for smaller businesses.

It's hard to imagine, though, while the British economy remains strong relative to that of the eurozone, that there would be any political incentive for it to join the monetary union.

The Sevso treasure is an example of a currency whose existence is inextricably complicated by human emotion, in the same way that attitudes to the euro often are in Britain (where the issue of the Queen's head on the coinage is often raised as if it were a matter of national security). The treasure was almost certainly discovered in Hungary in 1978. A copper cauldron about three feet across and one foot deep was dug up, packed with beautifully crafted silver plates, ewers, an amphora and a basin – at least fourteen pieces in all – dating from the Roman era. The cauldron was blackened by a cooking fire that had gone out more than 1,600 years earlier.

Estimates of the treasure's worth have been as high as £115 million, although doubt exists about its exact provenance. The man who probably dug it up – a young labourer called Jozsef Sumegh – was murdered and, it is supposed, the treasure stolen from him.

The Hungarian government claims it as its own, since it was apparently found on Hungarian soil.

But nearly everyone involved with this 'cursed' treasure has lied about its origins and obfuscated their murky dealings. For instance, both Lebanon and Croatia have claimed the treasure was dug up in their country.

When Sotheby's first tried to sell the treasure in 1990, on behalf of an English aristocrat called the Marquess of Northampton, it unwittingly illuminated something thought-provoking. Calculating that there were 29 modern countries that had previously formed the Roman Empire, Sotheby's decided to notify all 29 possible claimants in order to discharge its duty of 'due diligence'.

The attempted auction imploded in a cacophony of conflicting claims, and the sale didn't subsequently take place. This testifies to the measures that some people and governments will take in order to enrich themselves. Monetary unions, gold, silver, real or imagined, are as old as mankind – and so are their results.

# Many million fewer people speak German now than 100 years ago

The rise of the English language is the usual way of looking at this story. The internet, the economic and cultural dominance of the United States, and the residue of British influence abroad through organisations like the BBC gave English a head start over French in recent years – much to the chagrin of the French government and people. But the loss of German as an international language is much less remarked upon.

None of the German-language institutes I approached were prepared to make an educated guess at exactly how many millions fewer speak German now than in the decade before the First World War. But they confirmed that although the number of people who speak German as a first language has increased since 1945 – due to the growth of the Austrian and German populations – as a second language, German has dwindled away.

It's often said, by those who have tried, to be a difficult tongue to learn. Mark Twain wrote an essay on the subject called 'The Awful German Language' after taking nine weeks of lessons. But people don't often learn a language just because it has a reputation for being easy. Unavoidably, languages are highly political because they are a symbol of the culture from which they spring.

The EU has twenty official languages as a result of the enlargement in 2004. They are: Czech, Danish, Dutch, English, Estonian, Finnish, French, German, Greek, Hungarian, Italian, Latvian, Lithuanian, Maltese, Polish, Portuguese, Slovak, Slovene, Spanish and Swedish. At least seven of these language groups used to include a significant number of second-language German-speakers as a result of the Austro-Hungarian Empire, which disintegrated after the First World War.

Once upon a time, this central European entity stretched along Germany's eastern border, including some of the former Yugoslavia, the Czech Republic, Slovenia, Poland and a bit of Ukraine. The Austro-Hungarian Empire was allied with Germany and German was the largest single language grouping: around 10 per cent spoke it as a first language. To this day there's still periodic evidence that Germany sees some of these countries as client nations. For instance, in 1991 it outraged international opinion by unilaterally recognising Croatia as an independent state. This was Germany's most assertive foreign policy act since 1945 – and, unfortunately, one which fuelled the Balkan conflict.

These days, every EU citizen has the democratic right to be told in their first language what the EU is doing on their behalf. In terms of accountability, what could be more important? A cry frequently goes up that the money spent on translation services within the EU is too high, at about £545 million a year. But it's more important that each country can send its experts to Brussels to take part in discussions via interpreters, than that each country sends its best linguists to muddle through on subjects about which they know nothing.

One of the disadvantages of running a political organisation in which democracy, not to mention courtesy, demands the use of interpreters, is that it severely curtails the cut and thrust of debate. For instance, there was an incident in which Silvio Berlusconi, the Italian Prime Minister, insulted a German Member of the European Parliament (MEP). During a debate, Berlusconi compared the MEP to a concentration camp guard. The MEP didn't realise he was being insulted for several seconds while the translation took place, and when he did he simply removed his headphones and left.

There's an EU body called the Directorate-General for Translation, which deals with all translation and interpretation matters. Something akin to panic ensued there in 2004 when ten new countries joined the EU, nearly all of them with their own language. A competition to find Maltese linguists initially resulted in a complete blank – no one was employed. And in the cases of the former Soviet bloc countries, the EU encountered a particular problem for the first time.

Because these countries had been closed societies for 50 years or so, there had been no call for foreign languages and, as a result, there was no profession called 'translation'. Finding people who had a gift for languages and an interest in the job in countries such as Slovenia and Hungary turned out to be the bureaucratic equivalent of worm-charming. The lack of direct translators – for instance, fluent in Maltese–Slovenian – means that these languages are generally translated into English, French or German and then re-translated into a third language.

Much of the former Austro-Hungarian Empire was absorbed into the Communist bloc following the Second World War, resulting in the slow death of German as a second language – Communist governments often described it as 'the language of fascism'. This, together with Germany's unpopularity everywhere else immediately after the war, resulted in the decline of the language's international profile.

This is all the more poignant when you consider that Austria and Germany today constitute the largest single language block in the EU at around 90 million people. Yet the battle for linguistic supremacy has been between English and French. Of the 453 million people in the EU, roughly half of them now have something that can pass for a second language. Fifty per cent speak English, 20 per cent French and 20 per cent German. Shamefully, fewer than 5 per cent of Britons can even count to 20 in another language – the smallest number who can do so in any European country.

It may have been politically inevitable that the German language suffered this fate, but culturally it has been a tragedy for the rest of us. This chapter originally began as an attempt to investigate untranslatable words in European languages, but it rapidly became obvious that German has far more than its fair share of these, prompting the question: why?

Often German words and concepts are constructed by putting several smaller words together and this has facilitated the creation of many linguistic gems. But it also, for example, takes an unusually subtle public culture and mind to come up with *Schlimmbesserung*, which means a so-called improvement that has actually made matters worse. Or *Drachenfutter*, which describes a present that a guilty husband gives to his wife – a simple enough idea on its own, but given a kick in its tail by the fact that it literally means 'dragon fodder'.

'We tend to have this perception of German as harsh and guttural', said Dr Geraldine Horan, a German language expert at University College London. 'We have a negative preconception about German because of some of the sounds that are made. But it is romantic and beautiful as well. It is the language of Goethe, Schiller, Mann and Brecht. And from the 18th century onwards German played a very important role in shaping philosophical thought.'

'There is a very well-established philosophical area of the language in German and it is a very hard style of language to translate. It talks very much about abstract ideas and concepts and when you remove it from its original language there is very often the sense that you are missing something crucial – German is so dense and has so many meanings embedded in it.'

And so *Radfahrer* is one who has the dual habit of both browbeating his inferiors and toadying up to his bosses – although the word literally means 'cyclist', with its implication of the two things being opposite sides of the same wheel. And *Weltschmerz* describes a state of 'world grief', in which the world involved is a gloomy, romanticised version of the world most of us know. It's most often experienced by the privileged young, who consider themselves to be misunderstood geniuses.

*Bettschwere* is a state of consciousness too decadent and ponderous for anything except more sleep. It would lead you to remain in bed in a marvellous torpor, balanced between consciousness and unconsciousness. And *Feierabend* means the festive state of mind of a person at the end of the working day. Literally, it means 'celebration evening', as in: 'Honey, I'm home – and I'm full of *Feierabend*!' It might prompt one to go out drinking beer until bedtime, resulting in a *Katzenjammer* the next day, or a hangover of apparently terminal severity – the literal translation is the 'whinging and moaning of cats'.

The fortunes of a language are inextricably attached to its political context. So it could be argued that the whole point of the EU has been to pin the Germans into a framework in which they – and their language – are unable to dominate the continent as they have in the past. At least this language is worth the considerable effort.

# The Postojna caves in Slovenia are home to the Human Fish

Imagine an elemental rumble that lasted giga-years as the young Earth's minerals rolled over each other, reacting violently to implausibly bad weather and exploding out of the oceans before subsiding into the seabed again. Over a vast period of time, tectonic plates rubbed up against each other, mountains literally moved and the map of the world was re-ordered over and over again until it began to resemble the planet that we see today.

The Earth is – at our best guess – about 4.5 billion years old. The oldest parts of Europe, in Scandinavia, are reckoned to be 3.3 billion years. Much of the rest of northern Europe was probably formed 2 billion years ago and southern Europe was, relatively speaking, a geological afterthought, since it appeared roughly only 60 million years ago when sediments settled in the ocean between Africa and Northern Europe.

Around Slovenia, which is in the north of the former Yugoslavia, this sediment has a higher-than-average lime content. Over the last 2 million years, the limestone has been acted upon by carbonic acid in rainwater to create an intricate geology known as 'karst', and the outcome has to be seen to be believed. The caves at Postojna are a spectacular, bejewelled inner space under Europe's muddy skin. They are to be marvelled at, but – far more than the deepest forests of the surface – they also remind visitors that the veins and arteries of the Earth pump with forces that existed long before humanity. The caves are beautiful but not ultimately hospitable and the darkness that they incubate feeds primordial fear.

A Latin inscription over the entrance to the subterranean system says: *Immensum ad antrum aditus*!, or 'Enter, traveller, into this immensity'. Rather peculiarly, if you squint at the mouth, it's possible to see the outline of a sleeping face, as if the underground halls are waiting to be awoken by incautious visitors. So far, so Tolkien.

It's warm underground and, once away from the tunnel entrance, the air remains at a near-constant 10 degrees Celsius throughout the twelve-mile labyrinth. Only three of those miles are open to the public and there's always a drip, drip, drip of water falling between the roof and the floor – the metronome of history that created the caves and that will in all probability eventually also destroy them.

Once upon a time, well-to-do tourists and visitors were drawn through the tunnels in two-seater carriages. Later, when railway technology arrived in this corner of the Austro-Hungarian Empire, rails were laid and adapted for petrol-engine trains. But combustion engines in the confined space polluted the caves and discoloured the delicate membrane of the walls, which have white, silver and brown stone that glitters under light. Hand-held candles, straw torches and latterly electricity have been better sources of power for exploring the caves, and Postojna's tiny trains are now also electric.

Since they were first opened to the public in 1819, hundreds of thousands have visited these tunnels and they have played host to some of the sideshows of human Europe's biggest events. During the First World War, Russian prisoners built a bridge spanning one of the larger caverns, several of them falling into the blackness to their deaths during its construction. Then, when the country was under Nazi occupation during the Second World War, partisans detonated a German ammunition cache that was stored in the tunnels, doing to the structure of the place what geology would have taken millennia to accomplish.

It would be easy to reproach the impact that people have had on Postojna, were it not for the implacability of the caves' mineral nature: the partisans may have temporarily scratched its appearance but, as far as aesthetics go, whose loss is it but our own? The explosion may have altered the caves but, ask yourself, are they now more or less interesting to visit as a result? And what is the seeming-face at the entrance except a human construction put on something bigger than ourselves to make it less troubling?

Yet the caves are inextricably entwined with local history. There's a vast cavern known as 'the concert hall' – with room for 10,000 people – where world-class musicians, including Caruso, have performed. During the 19th century, it was known as 'the ballroom' because dances were held there at Whitsuntide, the stalactites and stalagmites illuminated each year in a blaze of noise and laughter.

Further along the usual tourist route, the shapes thrown by nature, its cathedrals of space and dangling spires, become even more phantasmagorical – piercing, melting and draping the air with outlines reminiscent of fabulous bells and domes. As if it were an inversion of man-made architecture, it's the atmosphere around the rock that seems to be doing the work: the usually insubstantial air soaring and plunging in such a way that even Gaudí's unfinished masterpiece in Barcelona, the Sagrada Familia, seems dully, conventionally *physical* by comparison. Whereas in Barcelona people are toiling to create something timeless, at Postojna it's time itself that's doing the work.

Every once in a while you see a sideways exit, an unlit doorway leading off into dark parts of the caves, unvisited by tourists. And then your guide turns off the lights for the 'experience'. Gulp.

As your other senses sharpen in the pitch-black, you think … could that possibly be the slap of clammy feet on stone in the distance? Is there a self-pitying muttering going on in the gloom? And what was it that the guide was saying earlier about a creature called the 'Human Fish'?

Eighty species of animal live in the Postojna caves, according to Professor Boris Sket, the leading academic associated with the caves. Speleobiology – the study of cave life – was born in Slovenia, where the need for it was, and is, self-evident. The university in Ljubljana, the Slovenian capital, has the world's best-known speleobiology department.

'The human fish is really neither', Professor Sket told me. 'It is a relative of the salamander. It is a small amphibian which can grow up to 30cm long and has no eyes. It is called "human" because it is the same white-pink colour as Caucasian skin.'

'It was first mentioned in scientific literature in 1689 as a creature that was believed locally to be a baby dragon. Every once in a while when it rained heavily, one or two would get washed out to the surface.'

'It has no eyes because it is adapted to life underground. Besides being totally dark, the underground environment is characterised by a relative lack of food. So any mutation that causes a reduction of unnecessary organs is favourable. This way natural selection is leading towards pigment reduction, eye reduction, etc.'

*Proteus anguinus*, to give it its Latin name, has been found blackened and burned by sunlight, suggesting that it's butting up against the forces of adaptation even as the speleobiologists look on: others have been found with eyes, foraging outside the caves.

Very unusually, the Human Fish also saves energy through a condition known as neoteny, which means that it becomes sexually mature without developing all the characteristics of an adult. It can breed as a small infant, which along with its sightless head, makes it creepy – like an oversexed finger on legs.

The Postojna cave system, where travellers choose to enter into something immense, is nature's operatic reminder of the powerful forces that are making and remaking the Earth and the fear that should characterise our relationship with them. The Human Fish is the icon of that fear: alien, weird and scuttling in the darkness.

# Turkey wants to join the EU but has 35,000 troops deployed for use against an EU member

The Greek half of Cyprus is looking down the barrel of a gun – or more accurately, roughly 35,000 of them, bristling from a Cypriot hillside. Despite having agreed to recognise Cyprus's membership of the European Union, Turkey maintains a heavy military presence on the north side of the disputed island. These soldiers are emblematic of the EU's difficulties in getting to grips with Turkey's 'European' identity.

European nations spent a large portion of the 20th century blowing hell out of each other and the European Union was invented mainly as a response to that destruction, with the hope of ending it. Turkey remained neutral during the Second World War. Yet why, by inviting it to become a member, would the EU invite military hostilities over its threshold in the form of the Greek/Turkish Cypriot debacle, when one of the main reasons for its existence is to avoid war?

Not only is Turkey still, at the time of writing, firmly embedded in Cyprus, but it also has an ongoing dispute with Greece involving an island called Imia or Kardek (depending on whether you regard it as Greek or Turkish) in the Aegean.

Most seriously, though, as a bar to its EU entry, there is the Turkish state's internal struggle with the Kurds. The Turkish security forces' efforts to centralise have created more than 300,000 Kurdish refugees. Try to imagine a Wales in which bilingual road signs and the S4C TV channel were illegal, and where villages in which anyone expressed a desire to be Welsh were immediately 'cleansed' from the map. Three thousand Kurdish villages in the south-east of Turkey have been systematically 'vanished', as a result of their desire for self-determination. If this is Europe, it is an old, atavistic Europe where today's Europeans no longer wish to live – and nor do the Kurds.

And yet despite these real, physical problems with Turkey's application to join the European Union, the tone of remarks made by leading West European figures quite often comes across as mere racism.

How adept we have become at reading between the lines when political leaders, such as Wilfred Martens speaking for the EU's Christian Democrat group, say things like: 'In our view Turkey can't be a candidate for EU membership. We are in favour of extensive co-operation with Turkey, but the European project is a civilisational project. Turkey's candidature for membership is unacceptable.' Now 'civilisational' is not a real word, even in translation. Did Mr Martens mean 'civilising' or simply 'relating to civilisation'? He left it fuzzy, perhaps because he was not clear himself.

Similarly the former German Chancellor Helmut Schmidt, a Social Democrat, said in a 1989 article for the German newspaper *Die Zeit* that Europeans are strongly characterised by a culture founded on a Christian tradition. Since Turkey, he added, is largely Muslim it belongs to a different cultural sphere: a sphere that lives in Africa and Asia. Yet there's nothing in the Treaty of Rome requiring member states to be Christian.

In 2002, Valéry Giscard d'Estaing, the former French President, said in an interview with *Le Monde*: 'Turkey is a country close to Europe, an important country, but it is not a European country. Its capital is not in Europe, it has 95 per cent of its population outside Europe.' Yet surely whether Turkey is – or will be – European is exactly the question at stake and one that politicians, including him, are in a position to influence. For him to say that 'Turkey should not be a member because I won't allow it to be' is a circular argument, and to define a political organisation geographically rather than politically is to miss the point. Also, considering that several Caribbean islands are members of the EU as a result of their association with France, one would think that a Frenchman in particular would be a bit more careful about taking such a position.

Turkey's geography is interesting, though. At a first, careless glance it appears to have no borders with present EU member states. Then you notice a small snip of land next to Greece and Bulgaria on the other side of the Black Sea strait, and detect a man-made bridge connecting the snip to the bulge of Anatolia.

Istanbul is on this 'snip', which has always been Ottoman, but by far the greatest length of Turkey's borders run alongside Iraq, Iran, Syria, Armenia and Georgia. While this makes it strategically important, it's not obviously, geographically, very European.

What does reinforce Turkey's European-ness, though, is its approach to statehood. Since 1923, when Kemal Atatürk founded Turkey on the ruins of the Ottoman Empire, the country has looked West for its political influences. Two years later, the state removed Islam as its official religion – a separation that made Turkey more like France than any other country in its secularist approach, and vice versa.

Since the Second World War, Turkey has joined all appropriate Western European inter-governmental programmes: the Organization for Economic Cooperation and Development in 1948, the Council of Europe in 1949, the North Atlantic Treaty Organization (NATO) in 1952 and the European Economic Community in 1963.

Of these organisations, Turkey's membership of NATO is the most significant, given that Turkey has an army of 600,000 – the second-largest standing army in the world after the United States. Turkey's strategic location as a bridge to the Middle East accounts for its brisk approach to military matters: any nation living next door to warring Ayatollahs, Saddam Hussein and various other appeasers of terrorism for decades would develop a robust attitude to force.

Turkey has long acted as a buffer for western Europe against the instability of the Middle East. It has kept itself armed to the teeth and largely ready to allow the Americans onto its soil, so that countries further west have had the luxury of arguing over whether they should send token troops to the region when trouble stirred. The Turkish government must regret failing to allow American troops to use it as a base for the 2003 Iraq war – especially since Turkey now has little influence over the future of the Iraqi Kurds as a result, and it sorely needed the financial aid package offered by the US in return for access to military bases.

The central role that the military plays in Turkish society and government, and the authoritarianism that this implies, help to explain the raft of domestic human rights problems that retard the country's EU application.

Human rights groups accept that the Turkish government has been trying, with some success, to turn around a culture of torture and extra-judicial killings among its security forces. But if the EU were more serious about Turkey's accession, there's much that it could do to help. For instance, it could provide forensic scientists – who are in very short supply in Turkey – to gather evidence of police torture that would stand up to scrutiny in courts and get those responsible imprisoned.

Turkey has been the victim of a double standard on more than one occasion: for instance, when it was leap-frogged by Slovakia for accession, despite similar human rights concerns about that country. Also, the EU's demand that Turkey should transform itself politically before discussing membership was unique among applicant states. Ordinarily the transformation embodied in the *acquis communautaire* (the checklist for aspiring EU members) is expected to take place alongside membership negotiations.

Perhaps Turkey's extra efforts are appropriate, though, because the implications of its becoming an EU member would be profound. The EU's influence in the Middle East would increase exponentially if it contained a large Muslim country, giving it a reason for a unified foreign policy of EU member states where currently it has none. France is against Turkey's admission at popular and political levels. Like France, Turkey is large and agricultural, and its accession would very likely make the inequities embedded in the Common Agricultural Policy finally unsustainable. France would be the biggest loser.

Ultimately, what's the *raison d'être* of the EU if it can't rise to the challenge of remaking Turkey in its own image? The real questions are: does Turkey want that? After that, what comes next? Iraq? And at what point – if any – would the European Union have to get itself a new name?

# When Estonia joined the EU, the price of sugar there shot up by 400 per cent

This also happened in the nine other countries that joined the EU in 2004 – on the world market a tonne of sugar cost only £135 but inside the European Union it cost £570.

Estonia felt the impact more than most because, since wriggling out from underneath the dead weight of the Soviet Empire, it has embraced economic liberalism with huge gusto. Low taxes and high growth in the world free market was its recently learned condition, so becoming part of the cosy, protectionist EU club was a change of lifestyle, to say the least. There must have been a lot of people who abruptly stopped taking sugar in their tea.

In Malta, Latvia, Estonia, Cyprus and Slovakia, some entrepreneurial types saw the price rise coming and stockpiled sugar – probably realising that it can be as addictive as nicotine (as well as, arguably, as dangerous). Once the European Commission had disentangled what had happened, it threatened them with fines, unless they fed their precious hoards to cows, or otherwise stopped 'distorting' the European sugar price with their white, granular hillocks. This is how protectionism works.

The Maltese EU Commissioner, Jo Borg, came out fighting. Brussels announced a special subsidy for his country, reducing the price to around £260 a tonne. The political opposition in Malta was quick to point out that, since the subsidy was paid for by EU taxpayers, the Maltese were effectively subsidising the lower price themselves. Borg snapped back that the Maltese ate far too much sugar anyway, and that – especially since 10 per cent of them were diabetic – they should stop moaning and read Professor Yudkin's book, *Pure, White and Deadly*, which attributes many common, modern causes of death to eating refined sugar.

The Common Agricultural Policy (CAP) determines the price of sugar (and all food) in Europe. It's often described as an arrangement designed by the French and Germans, under which France receives subsidies for its agricultural sector in exchange for buying

German-manufactured goods. With the apparently unstoppable rise of food processing, it's increasingly difficult to tell the difference between agriculture and manufacturing. But what's certain is that the CAP has made Europe what it is today.

An intricate network of tariffs and subsidies keeps food prices in Europe high in comparison with the rest of the world. European soil first encounters European money when the farmers who work it receive a direct EU subsidy. One growing season later, Europeans pay again when they purchase their 'expensive' food. And finally, Europe exports the food it doesn't need, in a process known evocatively as 'dumping'. Export companies receive a subsidy to compensate them for the money 'lost' by selling at the lower world prices, instead of to the lucrative European market.

'What is ironic is that the EU has two of the three biggest agricultural exporters in the world', said Eamonn Butler of the Adam Smith Institute. 'The US is the largest, followed by France and the Netherlands. And, contrary to public perception, European farmers are not merely inefficient toilers on tiny farms.

'There are two agricultural sectors in France. One is made of huge, highly efficient farms, and these are the French who ship meat, cheese and wine all over the world – but these farms employ very few. Then there are a huge number of people who inherited a tiny little farm from grandpa: a couple of fields, some geese and a cow. And these are the people who can be relied upon to go out on the street whenever the CAP is threatened.'

There's an international perception that French farmers wield a lot of power because we see them demonstrating and hear that the French government is sympathetic to them. But despite violent protests whenever changes to the CAP are proposed, the changes still take place whether small French farmers like it or not. Since the 1980s the most significant change has been that, rather than receiving money for the amount of food they grow – a system that produced wine lakes and butter mountains – farmers are now paid as 'guardians' of the land, sometimes receiving payments whether they grow anything or not.

This seems profligate at first glance and leads to anti-farming sentiment – particularly among city dwellers who, not always unreasonably, feel that since they have to get up and go to work on a train in the morning, it's wrong that others do not. But it's also work to maintain animal and bird habitats, build up hedgerows and prevent streams from bursting their banks. These farmers, although they don't produce food, keep the countryside in the form to which we have become accustomed. Without this tending, the land would become degraded – environmentally, visually and as an economic asset.

Many people also point to the damage that the CAP does to the economies of developing nations. Their market for selling sugar, for instance, is distorted by the EU and its money merry-go-round. Oxfam, in particular, produces regular reports on the world sugar situation and argues that the EU, as a responsible first-world body, should place the welfare of the developing world at the heart of its political aims. Instead, the EU currently 'dumps' about 5 million tonnes of sugar a year, lowering the price that farmers can get for their crops – in countries such as Mozambique, for instance, where life expectancy is only 38.

But to take this line is to misunderstand the nature of the European Union and the seriousness of its political intent. It's as much about realpolitik as is the Pentagon.

The CAP is not part of a 'mystical' relationship between farmers and their land: to say this is to deliberately obscure the point. Nor is there a conspiracy to keep rich farmers rich, hatched by a cabal of faceless bureaucrats getting backhanders, although doubtless this sometimes goes on somewhere.

As a result of the CAP – which costs between 40 and 50 per cent of the EU's budget – the countryside is a place where economic activity takes place in a broadly predictable way. It's not battered by the forces of world agricultural commodity prices, which are themselves subject to the most uncontrollable force of all – the weather.

Rural communities everywhere are typically poorer than their urban counterparts: it was ever thus. There's an economic phenomenon called the 'Engel effect', which says that when society at large gets more affluent, farmers – and the areas in which they live – often do not. This is because when people get richer they don't need to, and therefore do not, buy more food. Some people will spend a bit more on food and most will go to restaurants more often. But the extra money spent eating out goes to restaurant owners and other service industry workers: the price paid for the food remains roughly the same or tends to drop.

And where poverty is a force to be reckoned with, political instability usually follows. It was in the rural areas of Weimar Germany that Hitler was first able to get a toehold: poverty and desperation make people susceptible to predatory politicians. And it was the support of Russia's reviled peasantry that finally ensured the success of the Bolshevik revolution. One of the games that stupid tyrants play with each other is called 'create a large body of disaffected, starving yokels and then see what happens'. The results are never pretty.

Floods, famine, drought and resulting plague are something that most modern Europeans see taking place elsewhere, on television – and this is not only because the European climate is less severe than, say, Africa's. Historically, countless millions of Europeans have fallen victim to nature: some still do (think of the tens of thousands of elderly people who died across Europe in the 2003 heatwave). But these days we have back-up plans, government agencies and money, including the CAP, to minimise the impact that natural disasters have on Europeans, their food supply and their standard of living.

True, we pay more for our food than anyone else in the world. But because money that goes around also comes around, we can afford it. The flip side of financially supporting Europe's poorer areas (i.e. the countryside) is that the people from these areas can afford to lead modern lives and buy things, rather than scraping a subsistence living and appearing in newspaper photographs with flies on their faces when the harvest fails. The CAP has helped to create an affluent and welcoming European environment, in which pollution is rarely a problem and damage from 'natural' disasters – logging, for instance – barely gets a look in.

If the CAP were removed tomorrow, the cost of food would certainly drop. But then, probably, so would the price of land, and suddenly we would see precisely the economic upheaval and chaos that the CAP, and indeed the European Union, was designed to prevent.

## DID DAVID HASSELHOFF END THE COLD WAR?

Affluence and political stability make Europe a 'destination' – geographically and as a political organisation – that has countries and individuals queuing to get in. Essentially the CAP has made Europe what it is today.

# A Finn invented a free, widely available and – many argue – better alternative to Microsoft Windows

Microsoft is the largest company in the world. It made a profit of £21 billion in the year ending in June 2004, employs 55,000 people in 85 countries and in 2005 it allocated £3.5 billion for research and development. Its chief executive officer Bill Gates isn't only the richest man on the planet, he's probably also the richest in the history of the planet and its greatest-ever philanthropist. As of March 2004, he had given away £15.5 billion of his fortune.

This was possible because Windows is the operating system on 90 per cent of the world's computers: switching on, seeing the Windows logo and hearing its little sound-sunrise is one of the great international shared experiences.

In March 2004, the European Union found Microsoft guilty of abusing its near-monopoly and fined it £285 million for violating EU competition law in a case about the 'bundling' of Microsoft's Media Player with Windows. This would have felt like a rap on the knuckles for such a cash-rich organisation.

The argument went that because Microsoft had such a firm grip on the market for operating systems – the software that runs programs on personal computers – it could price out competing media players, reduce customers' incentives to check out alternatives and diminish the level of innovation within the market.

The EU's ruling followed a similar one in the United States about Microsoft's Internet Explorer. But on both sides of the Atlantic, the cases were brought not by customers complaining that Microsoft had curtailed their choices but by competitor companies scrambling for a share of the profits.

Some argued at the time that penalising Microsoft for its commanding position in this new market was really a tax on success. They pointed out that in less than twenty years the corporation had come to dominate by simply producing a product that most people wanted to buy at a price they could afford.

165

Bill Gates also raised the point that the products he sold were going to be obsolete in three years. By this time a better replacement would be on the market, so it was hard to understand how Microsoft's work could be construed as monopolistic behaviour in the traditional sense.

His detractors, of whom there are a great many, complained that Bill Gates and Microsoft were producing a mediocre product by programming standards, and using its consumer friendliness to bamboozle a public widely ignorant of the nitty-gritty of computing.

Part of this involved understanding the nature of the market. Microsoft achieved its success by using a different strategy to that of its main competitor, Apple, which branded its own product by using highly distinctive-looking hardware that was difficult to reverse-engineer.

Microsoft, on the other hand, made a decision to sell only software – the computer programs – and to leave the market for physical boxes and microchips to other companies. These companies could, and did, compete by producing relatively cheap products, thus making Windows more accessible to the thrifty man on the street than Apple, which was more aesthetically attractive but expensive by comparison.

This is where things start to get philosophically interesting. An operating system, like any computer program, is really just a series of ones and noughts arranged in a unique way – it's information. Moreover, it's information that is extremely cheap to replicate for the company that's selling it: how much does it really cost, once the programming work is done, to run off several million copies of a piece of software? The answer is not much.

The computer hacking community – people with the technical know-how – arose originally and largely out of academia because that is where most of the early computer programming was done. In the academic sphere, the sharing of one's work is routine – it's only through publication that academics can make a professional mark or contribute to the onward march of science and technology.

So it's hardly surprising that there was a political backlash within hacking sub-culture against the idea of 'proprietary technology' – Microsoft and other programs whose basic code was commercially and legally protected and unavailable to its users and business competitors.

Freedom of information is a basic tenet of an open society. Since computer technology is one of the biggest new markets in the industrialised world, much of which is composed of democracies, the availability or otherwise of computer codes to those seeking to innovate became a highly politicised issue.

In 1996, a young Finnish man called Linus Torvalds completed a masters degree in computer science at Helsinki University and produced a thesis called 'Linux: A Portable Operating System'.

His idea was that it would be possible to produce and make available an alternative to commercial operating systems. People could download this free of charge from the internet, with the basic codes also freely available for anyone who wished to tinker with them.

He made the idea a reality and it took off, firstly among his fellow hackers. He then attracted some heavyweight commercial backers who saw the advantage in challenging Microsoft's stranglehold. In 2001, IBM put £170 million into a three-year Linux development programme.

Linux has quite a few advantages over its commercial rivals – primarily, it's free. Since Microsoft's business plan had, ironically, brought down the cost of hardware, Linux has the capability to reduce the price of operating systems to a new low. Linux professionals working in small companies for customising and repairing systems will sometimes charge small fees, but these are dwarfed by the cost of buying and maintaining Windows.

Secondly, and this is perhaps the most important difference in the culture of Linux versus Microsoft, all the underlying codes are freely available. This means that the speed of innovation in Linux programming is held back only by the rate at which its many thousands of highly skilled computer-literate users can see potential improvements (while normal users can also install and run Linux without expertise).

Users discuss problems with the operating system openly on Linux web forums. This means that the public can solve them by tapping into a worldwide community of experts and without having to pay a corporate employee to do the work. The principle is that, since the operating system is available for nothing, users have a commensurate obligation to share knowledge of it.

Perhaps most surprisingly, Linux users are able to tap into Microsoft programs if they choose to, because Linux has the facility to store a complete replica of Windows inside itself, like a ship in a bottle. There are legal issues surrounding this, but the principle remains one of discretion. One can only speculate that, since most Linux users operate it in the privacy of their own homes, it's as much a question of getting caught as anything else. This alone puts a big question mark over whether Microsoft can really be considered to have a monopoly, since it's possible to use its products on an open-source Linux system.

Recently, Brazil announced that it's shifting its entire government computer network to Linux at a projected saving of £70 million a year. In Germany, the city of Munich will install the free system in the computers of 14,000 civil servants. And a report in the UK from the Office of Government Commerce in October 2004 concluded that changing to Linux software 'could generate significant savings'.

The idea of installing a different operating system on one's computer is daunting for the vast majority of PC users, so the home market probably has considerable stability as far as Microsoft executives are concerned. But it's harder to understand why more commercial organisations don't make the change – the savings generated for a large company could be competitively advantageous. IT departments are stuffed full of computer experts who run Linux at home on their PCs and would take the change in their stride.

More and more organisations will catch on to the extent of benefits gained through using Linux. Perhaps the days of commercial operating systems like Windows are numbered.

# In 1998, the Norwegian Prime Minister announced that he was depressed and took several weeks off work

'It had built up gradually over a long time', said Kjell Bondevik, who was writing his autobiography after a change of government when I spoke to him in 2005. 'I was sleeping fewer and fewer hours and felt that a wall was building up in my head. It was becoming increasingly difficult for me to lead meetings and I was trying to take long weekend breaks.'

'But then one weekend I more or less collapsed. I couldn't get up from my bed and everything seemed dark – even small problems seemed to be big problems. I called the doctor and he said that it was a depressive reaction. It had been brought on by a couple of different things.'

'Firstly, I had worked too much for far too long. I had been in Norwegian politics for 25 years and I never saw any limit to the work I could do. I had a good capacity, but every human being, as it turns out, has their limit. Secondly, I had experienced great personal losses in the time leading up to the collapse.'

'I lost my mother when she was far too young and then I lost a great many close friends my own age to cancer. In particular, four died of brain cancer and I had given myself no time to work with this. Grief is very tough and you need time.'

'The doctor was very good. I spoke to him every day for the first three or four weeks. Then, when I went back to work, there was also other treatment which I would rather not speak about. It was between myself and the doctor, but it was appropriate for me and it worked.'

'There are two reasons I issued the press statement about my illness. I hoped to contribute to the demystification of everything to do with depression and mental health. There is too much mystery surrounding these issues. And I also thought that if I didn't say anything there would be too much speculation about why I took time off – better to avoid speculation.'

Mr Bondevik was able smoothly to hand over the reins of government to his deputy and then, only three-and-a-half weeks later, he returned to work. He received more than 1,000 letters of support and comfort – many from Norwegians who had experienced mental health problems themselves and took courage from his example. If it could happen to the Prime Minister, then it could happen to anyone, right?

'I have learnt a great deal', he said. 'The way out of a depression is to talk about it, to your family and friends and in some situations also to a doctor. I learnt what a refined instrument the human body is and that it has to be treated with respect. And I also learnt about the need to set limits. When you have experienced the dark side of life you can better understand the good. I take far more pleasure now in the simple things: walking in the woods, having a long lunch with my family, listening to classical music.'

It's a straightforward story with a happy ending. At face value, it makes it hard to see why there's such a stigma about mental illness, since Mr Bondevik makes facing up to it seem easy. In particular, the story is heart-warming because it goes against the grain of what we think we know about politicians: it's hard to imagine most of them willingly admitting a weakness.

Mr Bondevik had the courage to be ordinary when the weight of usual political behaviour pressed in the other direction, and found that his decision was ultimately appreciated. But he probably felt as if he were in a cleft stick when deciding what to do. The public expects politicians to be both ordinary, by which is meant 'in touch', and extraordinary to justify their elevation as representatives and leaders of society. And the two things are ultimately incompatible in all but a very few people, making the relationship between electorates and their representatives extremely complex (and frequently mystifying when you see some of the people who achieve office).

For instance, the widespread mistrust of politicians is an odd phenomenon when you think about it. Since in democracies we vote for them – choose them ourselves – perhaps mistrusting them is as much an expression of self-hatred and mistrust of our own judgement as it is of not wishing to be told what to do. We frequently suspect that they present themselves as they would like to be seen rather than as they really are, and that their motivations for wanting office are impure. Why, we ask ourselves, do these people put themselves forward for a job that sounds rather thankless and dull? Worryingly, the inevitable conclusion is that they don't seem to be motivated by the same things as the rest of us – which, paradoxically, makes them unrepresentative.

Some work has been done on the psychology of politicians – mainly by Americans obsessed with POTUS (the President of the United States) and probably also with the eponymous power that he wields. But it's hard to discern in all the research what it is that these psychologists think politicians actually have in common with each other. The obvious factor is that they want the job, but the reasons for wanting the job may be legion: a sense of public duty, a hunger for recognition on the public stage, a sense of inadequacy leading to a need for affirmation, or an unrealistic sense of one's own importance, any combination of the above or something else entirely. After all, the theory in a democracy is that if you are unhappy with the job someone is doing on your behalf, you are supposed to do something about it and, perhaps, stand for election yourself. Is it too much to hope that this was a sufficient reason for a small handful of our MPs?

There are probably as many different kinds of political leaders as there are countries to be led because each electorate is different and expresses itself uniquely. Mr Bondevik, for instance, was an ordained Lutheran minister before he became a politician. It's hard to imagine, writing in the relatively godless United Kingdom, that such a man would find his way to the British House of Commons, let alone become Prime Minster. Churchmen in Britain have to get a free pass to the unelected House of Lords in order to make their presence felt in Parliament (and those unsettled by the fact that their government purports to represent them should consider how much more bizarre it is that churchmen in the Lords purport to represent God – especially if one doesn't happen to believe in him).

When it comes to mental health, though, we are all hypocrites. A large number of people experience depression – an estimated 121 million worldwide at any given moment, and the World Health Organisation projects that depression will be the second-largest burden of healthcare by 2020, after coronary heart disease. The usual figure given is that one in three people experience it at some point in their life, which makes it impossible for most of us to remain unaffected. Even if one is personally healthy, a family member is likely to suffer from it, simply by the law of averages, and so depression is one of the things that make us ordinary. Yet, even after Mr Bondevik, it's unlikely that we would look sympathetically on a representative who announced that he or she has sought psychiatric treatment, even – or especially? – for such a commonplace problem. If our representatives are going to be ordinary, we would rather, on the whole, that they show their ordinariness in a different way.

Winston Churchill had morbid depression his entire life, which he nicknamed his 'black dog', and Abraham Lincoln was similarly afflicted. But their possible bipolarity – in which deep depression can rapidly become high energy – is usually discussed in the same breath as their 'genius' and used as a reason why they were extraordinary, rather than ordinary. Also, it has to be remembered that Churchill was a contemporary of Franklin D. Roosevelt, who was in a wheelchair unbeknown to the American public by the time he died: all three great leaders existed in a time of lesser transparency that served them well. Who knows whether they would be elected today?

Ultimately it was the fact that Mr Bondevik did something so unexpected, by describing his taboo illness, that impressed his electorate (although it is doubtful that they would have remained impressed enough to let him keep his job if he had taken much longer to recover). It was the combination of his ordinary illness and his extraordinary job that worked rare magic to produce what's known as 'the Bondevik effect' in Norway today, akin to the Princess Diana effect or Bill Clinton's legendary ability to 'feel other people's pain'.

He created a moment of national catharsis and was rewarded for it politically, but the real test of his impact on the perception of mental illness is yet to come. If a second Norwegian Prime Minister had the same problem the situation would be far less extraordinary. Would it also be less welcome?

# Europe is harder to rebrand than soap powder – but not much

Advertising is not what it used to be. There was a time when 'Hey, wage-earner, buy these cigarettes. The real man's choice!' would do the trick. These days a jumble of semiotics on a hoarding, passing for art but projecting 'brand essence', is more normal. Silk Cut, Marlboro, Nike, Benetton, Gap and iPod. Once you get your head around the abstractions involved, this marketing tool can be applied to nearly anything.

The European Union has an image problem. There are many things said about it at a popular level, very few of them complimentary. And after the resounding No delivered to its constitution at the ballot box by the French and Dutch in 2005, it seems likely that the result was in large part because voters were influenced by their feelings for their national governments (who were advocating a Yes vote) – and the state of the world in general – rather than focusing on the question on the ballot paper.

To suggest that a stronger 'brand presence' for the EU might have produced a different result – which I suppose I am doing – wouldn't be elevating the superficial over the functional, for two reasons. Firstly, this isn't what good branding does: instead it takes the reality of the product and incorporates it into the message. A really successful advertising campaign can't be produced for a terrible product because it will get found out – the knack is to zoom in on the positive. Secondly, since nobody paid any real attention to the question of the constitution in the first place – in Britain, France or the Netherlands – a rebranding of Europe for British voters couldn't possibly reflect a departure from the status quo. But it might focus some minds.

Creenagh Lodge is the founder of Corporate Edge, a branding consultancy that has produced tourism campaigns for England, Ireland, Scotland and Wales, by recrafting their images in the international media. Her experiences have furnished her with an unusual insight into why British voters might choose to 'buy into' Europe at

173

the ballot box – or not. Europe is, after all, a place as well as a political project.

'There are two reasons why places are difficult to rebrand,' she said. 'We have done corporate rebranding for huge sprawling organisations. But however big they are, there are always still centralised structures: a human resource department or a communications hub that will allow you, when you have completed your exercise, to reach out to the guy in Ulan Bator, or the girl adding up the numbers in Tierra del Fuego and tell them what you have come up with.'

'But with countries, you can't get in touch with everyone when you're done and say: "This is what we are going to be about from here-on-in, this is what this company stands for. Have you got that?" You can't, for instance, tell the inhabitant of a region that if they don't agree with you they must move to a different continent. So it has to be done persuasively rather than coercively.'

'The second thing is that it takes a huge amount of time to change the reputation or brand image of a place: it's like turning a tanker around. For instance, in the case of Europe, people who weren't even thought of during the Second World War hold on to notions from then.'

In Britain, resentment towards Europe because of family history is not uncommon. If the first experience that a young man had of the place was clambering up a beach over the bodies of his dead mates on D-Day, it would leave a powerful negative impression on him and anyone to whom he talked about it. A rise in the affordability of foreign holidays means that most people have been abroad these days, but visiting Europe is not enough, on its own, to make you feel European.

What many Brits feel about Europe is that it's either a playground or a threat, possibly both. Huge numbers buy holiday homes abroad but don't necessarily think that speaking Spanish, Italian or French is important. Then they wonder why they have problems with lawyers, building regulations and so on. According to a recent EU survey, 65.9 per cent of UK residents speak only their native tongue, the highest level on the continent. Unlike other European schoolchildren, most Britons aren't really taught European history. Their encounters with the subject tend to be limited to stories about soldiers and sailors bashing up the French, Germans or Spanish. In our island story, the British are usually the scrappy insurgents, foraying bravely abroad on adventures and triumphing over the supposed sophistication of our continental rivals. Hurrah for John Bull!

But this isn't the only possible telling of the story. The idea of 'Christendom' could be one place to start.

The crusades were all about Christendom, which was basically another name for Europe. From the northernmost isles of Scotland and Norway all the way down to Istanbul or Constantinople, there was a time in Europe when this notion provided a very strong idea of being one civilisation.

In those days the only fully educated people were the monks, priests and clergy. They often learnt to be builders and architects and they moved around. So if you wanted to build a cathedral in, say, Birmingham, you would ask: 'Is Thomas of Ulm available? We like his work. Or Alfredo of Milan? How about him?' There was, literally, a freemasonry but also, as a result, a very powerful binding notion of what Christendom was.

Or an alternative starting point might be the later idea of the 'grand tour': the trip around Europe that became fashionable for aristocrats in the 18th century. You weren't anyone unless you had done it and bought the statuary.

But as a basis for presenting Europe to the British in a positive light, both these ideas contain problems. The concept of Christendom is difficult in a country as multicultural and basically secular as modern Britain, though it may have a strong romantic appeal to some. Also it excludes Turkey from the outset. In fact, to define modern Europe in these terms wouldn't be defining modern Europe at all.

Second, the grand tour was last seen on British television in costume dramas, as experienced by the landed gentry – powered, be-wigged and privileged – and it would be counterproductive to offer many ordinary Britons these 'toffs' as a prism through which to view Europe.

Class resentment is not specifically British, but an enduring sense of historical grievance and suspicion about the countryside – and the lack of dignity available for British labourers there – has led to many a class-based public relations debacle. For instance, no amount of self-deprecating humour will convince the average urban Brit that fox-hunting is a harmless pastime enjoyed by a broad cross-section of society.

In Britain, after the Enclosure Act, the smallholder ceased to exist. Either he went to the cities or he became a landless labourer, owned nothing and had nothing. Yet on mainland Europe, the smallholder lives on. Even now, in Normandy, you come across farms of three fields, in which each field has a little orchard, there's some watercress growing in the stream and there are a couple of cows and geese running around. Agribusiness is there too. But nevertheless the dignity of being a smallholder has endured for ordinary people in the countryside.

One might speculate that this is the reason why Continental food has historically been better than food in Britain, with a greater variety of fresh ingredients widely available. Otherwise, why should one country have rotten food (until recently) and all the other countries of Europe have had civil wars, world wars and been smashed to pieces repeatedly, yet still have regional cheeses that are made and appreciated?

In the US, by contrast, the working man's culture is closer to Britain's, encompassing shopping malls, gas-guzzling cars, zillions of television channels and the idealisation of small-town life. Jacques Chirac once issued a thank you to the British who go to small towns and villages in France to buy a second home, keeping the buildings from crumbling away, while the French prefer to live elsewhere. Maybe he was being ironic. Who can tell?

But although we may enjoy doing up ramshackle farmhouses in Normandy, it doesn't necessarily mean that the British feel at home with the locals, can speak the language proficiently or are ready to lose their historic prejudices about 'abroad'. So anyone trying to persuade the British to throw in their lot ideologically with the rest of Europe has a big task ahead of them.

Ms Lodge suggests an alternative approach. 'The easier route for a government trying to get a Yes vote would be to take the opportunity to say what Europe in the 21st century is all about. Not to bang on about the history, not to dwell on Christendom or the grand tour, although it is our ideological hinterland.'

'To successfully campaign for Europe, you would need to look for co-ordinating values in contemporary European and British society – "We stand for humanity. We stand for human rights."' Trade unionism could play a role – many of the recent improvements in workplace rights have come from Europe, though it doesn't often get the credit.

Creenagh Lodge would pitch Europe as 'the playground of the world, not just of Britain', with everything from ravishing ancient buildings to very exciting music. She would do it in such a way that Britain, with its lively, modern culture, played a starring role – as the jewel in a European crown.

'It would not be an all-time brand, simply a statement that would be attractive to ordinary Britons. You would be looking for something that would make people say: "Yes. I suppose I always knew that. And if that's true, I'll vote for it."'

But it would be a challenge of awesome proportions to take the task on at all. Despite brave words to the contrary, it's hard to imagine that the British government didn't heave a collective sigh of relief when the French and Dutch made a European constitutional referendum pointless ... for the time being.

# Snails are a type of fish under EU law

In 1989, Andrew Pearce, a Member of the European Parliament, asked the European Commission: 'In terms of community policies, are snails classified as fish or meat?' Slightly less than two months later, the answer came back – snails, other than sea snails (for some reason), are fish.

Mr Pearce is now unable to remember why he asked the question – it's not as if the snail industry is booming in suburban Cheshire, his former constituency. But it does illustrate how a bureaucracy can create its own reality, *à la* Kafka.

When you drop an edible snail into a bucket of salt water it fizzes slightly and then drowns. It might survive a little longer in fresh water, but it wouldn't be quality time. 'It makes no biological sense classifying snails with fish', said Professor Steve Jones, who knows more than the average man about both, having spent 30 years studying them. 'Fish are vertebrates and snails aren't. Fish are bilateral – they have a left and a right – whereas snails are built on a circular plane. And snails are hermaphrodite.' Case closed.

So what was the Commission up to, taking this position? Was it trying to squeeze euros from the Common Fisheries fund into the pockets of rapacious French snail farmers?

Apparently not. According to the Common Fisheries office, no snail farms receive subsidies. Edible snails are very popular – the French alone eat 40,000 tonnes a year – but 90 per cent are imported from Eastern Europe, and there's no record of a snail farm ever receiving a subsidy.

So why re-classify a land mollusc if there's no application for the information? The Common Fisheries people say that they have no idea why they bothered categorising snails as anything, adding that it's possible it happened only in response to Mr Pearce's initial question, more than fifteen years ago.

This wouldn't be out of character for the EU. Recently a Commission document, labelled 'To regulate or not to regulate', made the ground-breaking suggestion that officials should sometimes consider the option of 'doing less'. 'The option of no EU action should always be considered', it said, hinting that some of what it currently does is unnecessary. Classifying snails as fish may well fall into this category. What do you think?

But there's also another possible explanation for the story. A young journalist called Boris Johnson was the first to write about 'snails are fish' when he was the *Daily Telegraph*'s Brussels correspondent; he is now a Conservative MP. He wrote: 'A parliamentary question of this kind, involving translation into the nine languages of the EEC, involves spending about £1,000, and in the interim Mr Pearce lost his seat.' It was one of those pieces in which British newspapers specialise: ridiculing the European Commission without explaining the basis for the antipathy.

When I rang Mr Pearce to ask him about the story, he behaved as if I were trying to trap him or make him look foolish: he refused to explain why he had asked the question, and told me that all journalists were the same. He reserved special bile for Boris Johnson, who seems to have been largely responsible for his dislike of reporters.

Although it would be hard to prove since neither of them would talk to me, perhaps Johnson put Pearce up to asking the daft question of the Commission, with the intention of illustrating the EU's financial waste, which would have suited the *Daily Telegraph*'s Eurosceptic position. In the meantime, Johnson may have hinted at the paper giving a positive write-up of Mr Pearce's forthcoming election campaign. So when the Euromember for Cheshire lost his seat, he would have found no solace in being ridiculed in this same paper.

Even if the truth is some variation on this, the story – snails are fish – is symptomatic of why the EU is so little understood in Britain – a problem for which the media has a big share of responsibility.

Over and over again, when I told people that I was working on this book they would look knowing and say something like: 'Aha! Straight bananas and metric martyrs, eh?' – because these are the Europe stories that they remember.

The British press has done an amazing job over the years of managing to make the entire EU project appear frivolous and dull at the same time, which is quite an achievement. This is partly through laziness – it's easier to knock something than to explain it. But also because the genius of Britain's red-top tabloids lies in their ability to write a hilarious headline, and by their nature headlines don't contain a lot of information.

Newspapers are basically businesses selling the public what it wants. Far from leading public opinion, they often follow it, trying to anticipate what readers will want to think on any given subject. If there has been a persistent silence on the purpose of the EU, this is probably because there has been no great public hunger for the information or, at least, because there are many other things British people would rather read about.

Also, the nature of news is overwhelmingly negative: the definition of a story is something surprising, and this usually involves something going wrong. The EU has become established as the status quo (which is very confusing for Eurosceptic conservatives), and, in the public mind, as an organisation that's run by a bunch of odd foreigners, many of whom are French (break out the hilarious Frog jokes). Because of this, it has sunk quietly into the background and become an easy, cheap target.

By way of illustrating the difficulties involved in finding positive information about the EU in the British media, here is a tale …

On 28 January 2005, two independent reviews of the BBC's reporting of EU affairs were released. The *Daily Telegraph* ran the headline 'BBC cleared of EU bias but told staff need a shake-up'.

The article went on to say that staff, including ill-briefed presenters and junior researchers, lacked knowledge about the EU 'at every stage' of the BBC's news-writing process. The review, which had been commissioned by the governors of the BBC, investigated whether the BBC was 'systematically Europhile', an accusation of which it was cleared. But the picture that was uncovered was worse.

The *Telegraph* reported: 'There was a serious problem with all parties of various shades of euro-opinion feeling the coverage was not impartial. Sometimes being attacked from all sides is a sign that an organisation is getting it right. That is not so here. It is a sign that the BBC is getting it wrong.'

'Ignorance among BBC journalists needed to be addressed as a matter of urgency [and] there was a widespread perception that it suffers from certain forms of cultural and unintentional bias. There were problems at both ends of the [political] spectrum of reporting on the EU, with coverage on its enlargement having focused too much on fears of mass migration.'

'On the other hand', the report said, 'there was evidence of distaste for conservative ideas' among those involved in the news-gathering process, resulting in more complaints from Eurocritics than Europhiles. 'The inquiry found evidence of an institutional mindset when it came to the EU, but concluded that was not the same as deliberate bias.'

Now compare this with the headline in London's *Evening Standard* on the same day: 'Reports accuse BBC of bias in EU coverage.' Two stories, two diametric versions of the truth.

If BBC journalists are ignorant about Europe, what hope is there for the population that they are supposed to be informing? And in the British media the problem is compounded by newspapers that put their political agendas first: it's hard to see what factual basis the *Evening Standard* could have for its headline when at least one of the reviews said the exact opposite. On the other hand, the *Evening Standard* has a history of antipathy towards the BBC.

Everybody would like to believe that the information they receive is impartial. But on the subject of the EU, impartiality has remained elusive, for the simple reason that you can't approach it in a vacuum. You need a context in order to tell whether reporting is fair, and the debate in Britain has simply not been big enough to make that possible.

Snails may well be fish in Europe, as far as we know. Given the holes in our knowledge about the place, it wouldn't be entirely surprising.

# Two solar scientists bet a British climatologist $10,000 that the Earth will have cooled down by 2017

James Annan is an energetic young British climatologist working at the Frontier Research Centre for Global Change in Japan. His views about global warming and carbon dioxide ($CO_2$) emissions are mainstream: he subscribes to the idea that increased $CO_2$ emission by people and their industry is forcing up the surface temperature of the Earth. But he became frustrated with hearing opposing scientific views that appeared to have little in common with the reality he recognised.

These 'maverick' views and others like them were cited by the US government when, for instance, it failed to ratify the Kyoto agreement to control $CO_2$ emissions, so the stakes were high. As a way of resolving this frustration, Annan became interested in the work of Robin Hanson, an American academic, who invented the concept of 'ideas futures', a method of aggregating seemingly intractably opposed opinions. 'Any market transaction is essentially a bet, with the buyer betting that the price of an asset will rise, and the seller indicating that it will fall', said Annan. 'Hanson argues that by setting up a betting market in arbitrary questions, we can reach consensus positions much more reliably than by relying on panels of experts. The comments of some of these dissenters have been so absurd that I couldn't believe that they were made in good faith. Challenging them to a bet was a good way of establishing whether they really believed what they said.' In other words: are you serious enough to put your money where your mouth is?

In August 2005, Galina Mashnich and Vladimir Bashkirtsev of the Institute of Solar-Terrestrial Physics in Irkutsk, eastern Siberia, took him up on his offer. Their research has led them to believe that sunspot activity is about to enter a 'less active phase', which will bring about cooling of the Earth over the next few decades. Specifically the bet is that the average global surface temperature between

2012 and 2017 will be lower than between 1998 and 2003. If the temperature drops, the Russians get US$10,000 (£5,700) from Annan and vice versa. It should be clear relatively soon who will win – in less than ten years the jig will be up, and in the context of climate change this really is very soon indeed.

In his book *A Short History of Nearly Everything*, Bill Bryson produced a layman's summary of the scientific history of the Earth. He managed neatly to sidestep the global warming debate by focusing on the bigger picture, describing the work of scientists whose theories are still accepted as relevant and sketching what's known about the ups and downs of the Earth's climate over many millions of years.

He describes how, for instance, about 12,000 years ago the Earth began to warm, then plunged back into bitter cold for a thousand years or so. After this, average temperatures leapt again, by as much as four degrees Celsius in twenty years – much more than the biggest change predicted for our immediate future. And this was all pre-Industrial Revolution, so these changes took place independent of any human contribution.

'What is most alarming is that we have no idea – none – what natural phenomena could so swiftly rattle the Earth's natural thermometer', Bryson wrote. 'Climate is the product of so many variables – rising and falling $CO_2$ levels, the shifts of continents, solar activity, the stately wobbles of the Earth – that it is as difficult to comprehend the events of the past as it is to predict the future. Much is simply beyond us. Take Antarctica. For at least 20 million years after it settled over the South Pole, Antarctica remained covered in plants and free of ice. That simply shouldn't have been possible.'

Thanks to ice cores extracted in Greenland, we have a detailed record of climate for the last 100,000 years, yet climatologists have had very little success explaining global changes in temperature and conditions. The best way to do this these days is with computer modelling. This involves testing theories by inputting data about what we know actually happened and then seeing whether what occurred next would, in fact, have taken place if the theory were correct. This is possible because there are large amounts of data to test the theories against.

But none of it has worked very well so far – the science is still in its infancy. So ask yourself this: given that the scientific community has had very little luck explaining past changes despite all the data, how likely is it that theories about the future are correct, when by definition there's no solid data yet?

Also, how can there be such a strong consensus among scientists about the warming of the Earth in the future when so little exists about climate changes in the past? It's one thing to observe, by looking at a thermometer, that the temperature is rising but another entirely to figure out why.

I became interested in the subject when trying to write a piece for a British newspaper about how several parts of the globe were cooling down rather than warming up. It was clear that this was the case from looking at a map produced in 2001 by the United Nations International Panel on Climate Change (IPCC), which is regarded by many as the ultimate authority on global warming.

The map was available on the internet as part of the latest UN report on global warming, so the cooling patches were there for everyone to see. They were relatively small and therefore couldn't be very significant in the grand scheme of things, I thought. After all, when climatologists send us repeated warnings about global warming they must have looked into the anomalies (the exceptions that prove the rule). I assumed that the cooling patches would be general knowledge to climatologists. I was wrong.

I spoke to about 25 of them from all over the world, being passed from one to the next when each found that they were unable to help me. With only two exceptions, the fact that certain areas were cooling down had entirely escaped their attention: they all thought it was interesting but had no idea why they should exist. Once they knew about the cooling patches a couple suggested that it may be to do with the ocean – all the patches were on the west coasts of major continents – but both pointed out that very little was known about how the world's oceans affect climate. 'But', I asked, 'two-thirds of the planet is covered with water and some of it is really deep. How is it possible to rule out the ocean, or something in it, as a cause of climate change when so little is known?'

I got the telephone equivalent of a shrug from four continents. To a layman, even at a cursory glance, there seem to be quite a few holes in mainstream climatology theory. For instance, why did global warming (commonly attributed to human impact) begin only in 1975, according to the IPCC's graphs – when the human Industrial Revolution began 300 or so years before?

And if, as it's claimed, the planet had simply reached a 'tipping point' after a long build-up of $CO_2$ for many years, why did no one anticipate it?

Is it possible that climatology is a science that has come about mainly in response to the phenomenon of global warming? And if this is the case, then what interest does it really have in examining its own most basic premises?

What's clear, though, is that taken seriously, climatology is a hugely complex science with many variables. The pay isn't good because – unlike space, weapons technology, computing, or anything with a commercial application – there's no money in it, so perhaps it doesn't attract the same grade or number of applicants as disciplines with greater rewards. But in the long term, the work that is being done is hugely interesting and valuable in a wider, if not in a financial sense.

So far, two lonely solar scientists in eastern Siberia are the only takers for James Annan's bet about the weather and they stand to be vindicated or mocked in 2017. But it's also apparent that Mr Annan is one of only a very few people who has stepped up to the challenge financially on the mainstream side of the debate either. He has a theory that the debate isn't really to do with the weather at all, but is instead about human psychology: left-wing versus right-wing opinions, precautionary versus risk-seeking behaviour, or preferring government over a free-market solution to a problem.

But I wonder whether the reason why there are so few climatologists involved in Annan's experiment is that they have a much better sense than the rest of us how little is really understood about the subject.

# On being told that there was an Austria–Hungary football match on television, Otto von Habsburg asked absentmindedly, 'who are we playing?'

In 1919 the Austro-Hungarian Empire folded, and after 600 years of dynastic rule the Habsburgs could be said to have taken it quite well. Following a short-lived attempt to reclaim the family 'birthright', the Emperor-King Charles died of pneumonia in Switzerland in 1922 and his son Otto emigrated to the United States with his mother.

In 1951, Otto married Princess Regina of Saxe-Meinigen and they settled in Pocking, Bavaria, where their large house came to be known by the locals as 'Pockingham Palace'. Then in 1961 the middle-aged Otto renounced his title as a member of the House of Habsburg-Lorraine and all accompanying claims to sovereignty. He had his reasons.

Europe is teeming with down-at-heel royals with similar stories to tell. The relatively healthy British monarchy is related to most of them via Queen Victoria and her extremely large family: the Habsburgs are their cousins, as are the Saxe-Coburg-Gothas of Belgium, the Hohenzollern-Sigmaringens of Romania and the Savoys of Italy.

They can be seen as living history: their haemophiliac bloodline linking directly to a past in which nations were led by individuals allegedly chosen by divine providence and with a mystical connection to the land.

Three hundred and fifty years after the execution of Charles I of England and 200 years after the execution of Louis XVI of France, eight European countries have monarchs as their heads of state. Each of Europe's historically elastic borders was once the demarcation line of some kingdom or empire, with the ebbs and flows of international relations reflecting the political health and wiles of the respective monarchies.

Prussia is a case in point: it used to be an area in central Europe dominated by Protestant north and eastern Germany. It included parts of lots of other modern countries, including a large chunk of Poland, and was ruled by a landed aristocracy known as *junckers*.

In the mid-19th century, Otto von Bismarck set about trying to make Prussia into a modern nation-state. Being a *juncker* himself he had an interest in maintaining the status quo – at least in as far as who held the reins of power – and he was regarded by many as a uniquely effective Prime Minister.

But the Prussian monarchy – the House of Hohenzollern led by Wilhelm II – got nervous of the power that Bismarck wielded and dismissed him. This gave them a free hand to lead Prussia, or Germany as it had by then become, into the First World War. The disastrous outcome, however, forced the monarchy to step aside and Germany is now a republic.

In a more successful vein, in 1975 King Juan Carlos rose to the throne of Spain after the death of Franco, who had been its fascist dictator since the civil war of the 1930s. The King provided some continuity at a time when it was desperately needed, and championed democracy when some of Spain's military tried to kill it again in 1981. By nearly anyone's standards, this makes Juan Carlos – as they would say in that other bowdlerised history book *1066 and All That* – 'A Good Thing'. So generalising about the role that monarchy has played in modern European politics is not altogether very fruitful.

When you pull back from politics, you can look at monarchy as an oddly European cultural phenomenon. Go into any well-stocked newsagent, gaze along the shelves and you will see glossy rows of magazines containing photographs of aristocrats and royals. Forget the claims that celebrity has replaced royalty – royalty is still there and John Locke, the British philosopher who first opposed the idea of the divine right to rule, is probably heaving in his grave.

These days, we don't spend much time musing how European life is free from the tyranny that a bad monarchy can inflict on its people. But we are far more likely to be found tittering that Zara Phillips of the British royal family has a tongue stud and enjoys rolling in hay with stable boys, or marvelling that Prince Frederik of Denmark married an Australian estate agent.

On the announcement of Prince Charles' marriage to Camilla Parker Bowles, *The Times* newspaper made a neat point. Casting around for a new angle on an old story, it came up with Uberto Omar Gasche, a man with a very large moustache and a keen interest in nude photography and mastiff hounds.

Were it not for a quirk of history, the paper said, this eccentric Italian aristocrat would be the United Kingdom's future monarch rather than Prince Charles. Specifically, it was the 1701 Act of Settlement (which prevented British monarchs marrying Catholics and gave male heirs priority over their sisters) and three centuries of elapsed time that stood in the poor man's way. How better to demonstrate the random nature of monarchy? If the harvest had failed, perhaps Signor Gasche could have taken some nude pictures of his dogs?

Lots of European royal families fell by the wayside during the 20th century as a result of hubris and political incompetence. Yet the European Commission is based in the Kingdom of Belgium and the European Parliament in the Grand Duchy of Luxembourg.

Magazines like *Majesty* and *Royalty* may be perceived as catering to a minority of middle-aged ladies and filed alongside magazines about soap operas, but they exist. This may be because their readers are moved to look for something profound about the lives of these ordinary but rich Euro-folk, which is a highly traditional reflex and sign that democratic politics is a tiring thing.

Life is complicated but we'd like it to be simpler. A king or queen wearing a crown and ermine appeals to the dreamer in all of us – children's literature has always used princes and princesses as central characters to cater to each young reader's sense that they too are unique. However, in the real world it's certainly also true that some adults have a vested interested in maintaining the status quo. The emotional ties that we have with our past are many and complex, and royalty is one of the modern beneficiaries.

Equally, it's often said that history is written by its victors – to the point where it's a cliché. In 1979, after renouncing his claim to the throne of his father's empire, Otto von Habsburg took German citizenship in order to be eligible to fight in the European elections.

He became a deputy to the European Parliament for Bavaria and championed the idea that the European Union should expand eastwards, which was not a popular view at the time. He was especially keen that Bohemia, Slovakia, Slovenia, Hungary and Croatia – as well as Austria – should have the opportunity to join the EU, which would have had the effect of reuniting the former Habsburg Empire. Bohemia has since become a part of the Czech Republic, four out of the remaining five countries have joined the EU, and Croatia has applied for the next round of accessions – which would mean a clean sweep.

So history is written by its winners. Dr von Habsburg has published more than 30 books and his eldest son chose to take the title His Imperial and Royal Highness, Imperial Crown Prince and Archduke Karl of Austria – not bad for a family that was officially deposed in 1919.

There's a story told about an anonymous British Cabinet minister and Prince Willem-Alexander of the Netherlands. The minister once recalled to the Prince how, as a young Labour MP noted for his strident republicanism, he was introduced to Queen Elizabeth with other members of a committee. He had vowed that he wouldn't bow … but before he could finish the story Prince Willem asked: 'When you came face to face with your Queen, did she mutter something in a low voice, so that you had to bend forward to catch what she had said? And then did she move on down the line, so that to onlookers it seemed as if you'd bowed?'

Taken aback, the Cabinet minister asked how the Prince knew that that was exactly what had happened. In reply, the Prince winked.

The era of ruling monarchies may be over in a strict sense but the continent of Europe in all its imagined 'Old World' glory remains a set dressed for their continued existence – in their imaginations, in the pages of magazines and as a baroque part of our traditional, psychological landscape.

# In 1993, an EC official fell to his death from the top of a tall building in the centre of Brussels

The Rue de la Loi is lined with nondescript EU office buildings, and the fact that it's called the 'Road of the Law' gives extra piquancy to Antonio Quatraro's death there more than ten years ago. In March 1993 he plummeted from a top-storey window and landed on an escalator, the law of gravity being his final consideration.

Dr Quatraro was under investigation for corruption by internal European Commission auditors. He was involved in the sale of 'intervention tobacco', which was to the tobacco market what butter mountains and wine lakes were to food sales at the time. There was some evidence that he had been selling the stuff to Italian and Greek companies with mafia connections and taking bribes to do so – suspicions were aroused because many of the bids to buy the tobacco were written out in the same handwriting.

The matter was looked into further after his death, but it was found that there was no case to answer and that Dr Quatraro had acted alone. At least, this is the official version of events.

Several people have pointed out that Dr Quatraro would never have believed that he could get away with such an elementary scam had his superiors not made a series of recent changes to internal procedures (in particular, Martin Jay at *The Sprout* magazine in Brussels pursued this story with admirable relentlessness). There was also a strong and persistent rumour that Dr Quatraro had been seen out on the town with some unsavoury Italian characters the night before his death, but in the absence of a fuller investigation this is hearsay.

On the same day that Dr Quatraro died, he was mentioned on the floor of the House of Commons by Sir Teddy Taylor, during a debate on European Community (EC) finances. According to Hansard, he asked Bill Cash: 'Will my honourable friend have time to mention the appalling fraud in EC tobacco subsidies, which are costing more than £1,000 million, especially in view of the tragic information that we have received from the tapes half an hour ago, that the head of the tobacco division of the EC's agriculture department, Mr Antonio Quatraro, has jumped out of a window and committed suicide because he was alleged to have shown favouritism to Italian tobacco producers?'

More than twelve years later, it's believed that the Belgian police still list Dr Quatraro's as an 'unsolved murder'. It's hard to get them to return phone calls on the subject, although there's nothing especially odd about this because police forces the world over have bad press officers. Other journalists have been told that it's an unsolved murder and I have no reason to disbelieve it.

The toxic whiff of corruption around the European tobacco industry is one of several problems connected with the heavily subsidised sector. The EU is the world's fifth-largest producer of tobacco (behind China, Brazil, India and the US), spending £657 million on tobacco subsidies in 2002 – £5,183 for every tobacco worker in southern Europe – and only £9 million on anti-smoking programmes. If criminals are attracted to the sector then it is likely that they detect easy pickings. Disturbingly, the experiences of EU officials who have tried to deal with the industry also suggest that this is the case.

In 1995, a young accountant called Robert Dougal Watt was seconded to Luxembourg from the National Audit Office (NAO) in London. A Scottish Presbyterian, he had a history degree from Edinburgh University and worked for British Customs and Excise before training as an accountant with the NAO. Once in Luxembourg, he worked on agricultural subsidies for several years, made good progress, received a couple of promotions and by the summer of 2001 had become a Grade A staff member at the Court of Auditors. He was moved to audit tobacco subsidies.

'I was given a report to read that mentioned Quatraro ... There was a paragraph that just said something like "During the course of the investigation an official died"', Mr Watt told me. A bewhiskered, easy-going sort of person, four years on he still seemed bemused at the absurdity of coming across an unexplained death in an EC report about tobacco subsidies.

'I looked at this, wondered about it, picked up the report and went beetling down the corridor to my colleague's office to ask what it was all about – one of the things that you learn is that European reports can be a bit oblique.'

It's possible that he now wishes he'd never opened that report – once he began his investigation, he uncovered a series of scandals that led right back to his own employer, the Court of Auditors. His resulting allegations of nepotism and that the Court of Auditors had turned a blind eye to wrongdoing (including failing to investigate adequately Dr Quatraro's death), eventually led him to become a whistleblower, putting an early end to his career with the EU.

In April 2002, he complained formally to the European ombudsman, MEPs and court staff of 'systematic corruption and abuse in the European Court of Auditors' and produced a bulging dossier to back his claims. At around the same time, he stood in an election for a staff committee using his dossier as a manifesto, along with the suggestion that the entire Court of Auditors should resign. He won the support of around 40 per cent of his 500 or so colleagues.

Mr Watt believes that the Court of Auditors, which is supposed to be the European Union's anti-fraud office, misled investigators and the European Parliament about Dr Quatraro's death. The unfortunate man, he says, was 'not any Mr Big, but was more probably a minor and coerced player in a conspiracy within the European Commission'.

He claimed that corruption was 'permitted to flourish to the benefit of all the institutions' elites' and described the EU accountancy system as 'so degraded it can't police itself'. In July 2003 he was sacked.

And he is not alone. Marta Andreasen, a Spaniard who worked closely with Neil Kinnock, went in a very similar way, as did Paul van Buitenan, who worked in financial control at the Commission. They are simply at the top of a list of EU whistleblowers.

Each of these jobs represents someone's whole life. Given the kind of steady character required to pass the exams and interviews necessary to become one of the best-paid bureaucrats in the world, it's hard to imagine that any of them took the decision to become a whistleblower lightly.

When I met him in June 2005, Mr Watt was coming to the end of his severance money and had sold his car. He was trying to overcome the shock of being sacked – simply for doing his job – in order to present a good face at job interviews.

'It has been a very difficult time', said Mr Watt. 'And it wasn't helped much by the fact that they tried to classify me as a nutcase. I try not to be angry because I can see the internal logic of why things have happened the way they have. But if you have spent your working life trying accurately to describe reality – which is what an auditor does – it doesn't make you happy to see things deliberately obscured. I suppose I'm still livid.'

'A lot of my former colleagues regard what I did as extreme, because essentially I was blowing the whistle on things that they already knew about. But – and I think this is important to understand about the way that things work – whereas many of them had families to think of, I did not.'

'A lot of people who work at the Court of Auditors feel that, yes, some of their findings are twisted, obscured and hidden. But as long as some of the work gets through it allows them to sleep at night.'

Fortunately for the rest of us, whose money is being audited, not everyone takes this pragmatic view. Until the EU learns to treasure its whistleblowers rather than sack them it will remain an easy target for its political enemies, as well as criminals seeking to profit from lax controls.

# Padstow in Cornwall and Krakow in Poland have identical festivals involving hobby-horses

The story begins with a German biscuit. Peter Matthews, who is the managing director of Nucleus, a 'branding experience' consultancy on the outskirts of London, did some work for a German company called Bahlsen in the early 1990s. Their business was to produce biscuits and coffee and export them to the Soviet bloc, among other places.

Branding was unheard of in Eastern Europe at that time and the biscuits were known only as 'Bahlsen biscuits' in Poland, although unfortunately this was pronounced 'Belson' (like the concentration camp) and the biscuits cost up to a week's wages, making them something of a luxury item.

Mr Matthews was asked to help turn them into a household name. 'It was a very low-volume business and the idea was to build it up in its existing market', he explained.

'So we did a bit of looking around at the history of the company and Poland, and discovered that the people of Krakow were very proud of their past: there was a lot there we could use.

'When Genghis Khan's hordes were trying – and mainly succeeding – to conquer the world, they arrived at the gates of Krakow and the knights of the city saw him off.' It seems that in 1241 the Poles stood atop the walls of the town and shook their shields belligerently at the approaching Mongol army, only to be rewarded – and probably also a little bewildered – when the battle-hardened warriors simply turned around and left. It must have seemed especially odd since one of the reasons the Mongols were battle-hardened was that they had successfully sacked Krakow only a few years previously; they were unlikely to be overawed by the task at hand. Still, why look a gift horse in the mouth, the good people of Krakow probably reasoned?

To this day, they celebrate this famous victory every May. This involves someone dressing as a Mongol soldier, riding a hobby-horse and parading around the town centre to much sing-ing, dancing and drinking. The figure and the festival are called *Lajkonik* (pronounced 'laconic') after the knights of Krakow.

Nucleus decided to use the horse's head on the Bahlsen biscuit packet, rename the product 'Lajkonik' and make the packet very bright and cheerful because Polish supermarkets at the time were extremely badly-lit. The biscuits became a hit.

Mr Matthews paused in his retelling of this story and cleared his throat. 'But the actual history of the *Lajkonik* victory – which Poles don't generally accept – was that when the Mongol hordes reached Krakow they received news from a long way behind their line that their leader, Genghis Khan's son, Ogedei, had died. He had been a rather top-down commander so, unsure what to do next, the armies of the Khan simply turned around and went home, leaving the knights of Krakow to take the credit.' Still worth a party, surely, if only for the stupendous luck involved?

Slightly bizarrely, at first glance anyway, an identical festival takes place several hundred miles away, in the insular Cornish town of Padstow in south-west Britain. Known as the 'Obby Oss' – a Cornish pronunciation of hobby-horse – two wooden horses are paraded around the streets every May Day, carried by some of the seafaring town's burliest men, to the accompaniment of an annoyingly catchy song. It's supposed to be bad luck to sing the anthem on any other day of the year.

The origins of the Padstow May Day Obby Oss are murky. The rumour is that it's a fertility ritual related to Beltane, a pagan festival involving bonfires and free-for-all sex. Women who find themselves beneath the osses' skirts are alleged to become especially fertile and much is made of the 'teaser', who dances in front of the osses, leading them on, so to speak, by waving something that looks like a big hairbrush.

'I think it is fair to say that the origins of the Obby Oss are lost in the mists of time,' said the Reverend Barry Kinsman of St Petroc's church in Padstow, who is also a local historian. 'The only connec-tion with horses I can think of is that one of the verses of the song has a line "Where is Saint George?" who was obviously a knight. But other than that I really couldn't say.'

In fact, a little investigation revealed that there are less high-profile hobby-horse festivals in a whole clatter of places across Europe and farther afield. In Britain alone, Minehead, Salisbury, Symondsbury, Thanet, Abbots Bromley and Burringham all have one, as do Brussels, Namur, Malines and Dendermonde across the channel – pointing to a wider significance for the iconography.

In his book *Meditations on a Hobby-horse*, art historian E.H. Gombrich uses the child's toy as a good example of representative art: he says that there's no mistaking what a horse's head on a stick is supposed to be. It has no legs or body but the head clearly indicates what else we should imagine – and someone astride a hobby-horse is playing at being a knight.

This is also explicit in the British Library's online picture catalogue, where if you look up 'hobby-horse' you get two images, one from 15th-century India, showing children galloping about with sticks between their legs, and a second from an artist in 16th-century Bruges. This vibrant oil is of a tournament with knights in armour, jousting on horses wearing heraldic coats, with a prosperous medieval town in the background. In a strip along the bottom of the canvas is a separate, less colourful picture of children playing on hobby-horses, imitating their heroes ... or was the artist perhaps drawing a connection in the opposite direction about the childish nature of a jousting tournament?

So there are two annual festivals several hundred miles apart, separated by an ocean but united by an icon of a hobby-horse and whatever it means ... so here is a suggestion. Horses were extremely valuable at the time. They represented transport, status and self-determination in the same way that cars do now, but fewer people could afford them. Ridden by a knight, a horse was also a reminder of the power of its owner, a warrior who was intimately involved with the forces of life and death.

In Krakow, the hobby-horse and rider represent the warriors of the Mongol army and also the knights of Krakow who 'defeated' them. It's a Mongol, rather than Polish, knight on the hobby-horse to remind onlookers which historic Polish battle they are commemorating.

The closest that the Padstow Obby Oss ever came to being in a battle was, legend would have it, when a French ship was spotted off the coast, probably in the 18th century. The people of the town dressed up in red cloaks and marched across the cliffs with the Oss – who was already a May Day feature – carried ahead of them. The way that the Cornish tell it, the French mistook the crowd for a British redcoat force led by the devil and sailed off. But it's entirely possible that, like the Mongol hordes at Krakow, the French simply had better things to do.

At Beltane the Padstow Oss might very well be a representation of something sexual, as much as it's about St George or any other figure of authority riding around with a strapping great sinewy horse's neck poking out between his legs – the symbolism is explicit and power is a notorious aphrodisiac.

So next time you see a line of little girls out pony-trekking, spare a thought for the subconscious considerations. Horses, and the people who historically had the money and reason to own them, ride on in the popular imagination – even in these mechanised days – because money, sex, war and power are universal human pre-occupations with symbols that change very little. Doubtless the shape of a Panzer tank and a soaring fighter jet will live on similarly in the popular imagination for as many centuries, even after they are militarily redundant. The Padstow and Krakow festivals – and many others across Europe – look the same for this reason.

DID DAVID HASSELHOFF END THE COLD WAR?

# Skoda means 'shame', 'damage' or 'pity' in Czech

How's that for a piece of branding? It gives other Skoda jokes a run for their money. But the company is nearly 150 years old and the name wasn't chosen as a result of a marketing exercise. Nor has the name been a problem, for several reasons; the first being that once upon a time there was a Mr Skoda.

Born in 1839 in Cheb, Emil Skoda was 27 when he became head of the Pilsen Machine Works. He showed outstanding managerial ability and in 1869 bought the factory from his boss, Count Arnost Waldstein, after a period of lacklustre business brought on by the Austro-Prussian war.

He named his factory after himself and spent the next few decades diversifying. Young Emil, by this stage, had ceased to be young and had been made a lifetime member of the Czech parliament. By 1914, Skoda was the major arms manufacturer to the Austro-Hungarian Empire.

So Mr Skoda's success belied his family name, which, like most, had its origin in the remote past. Many Czechs are named after objects or emotions and it's not uncommon, I'm told, to come across a Mr Magpie, a Miss Ceiling or a Mrs Unbearably Happy in a Czech phone directory. According to David Short at University College London, Skoda is one of a cluster of names that arose in Czechoslovakia around four or five hundred years ago because their original bearers encountered a notable setback or success in business or agriculture. Other Czech surnames in this category include Koista, which means 'someone who did very well, probably at the expense of someone else'; Vajdlek, which means 'a nice little earner'; and Nouza, which means 'war, want or woe'. So perhaps the manufacturing company that took young Emil's name could have fared worse.

To Czechs these days, the word Skoda registers mainly as 'a successful business' and to other Europeans as 'a cut-price Volkswagen', after the German car company took it over in 1991. Skoda may have a lemon of a name in modern marketing terms but it hasn't mattered. Whatever marketing executives would have you believe, there used to be – and perhaps still are – forces in life more important than advertising, branding or marketing.

Back to the story of Skoda then. In 1945, the company was nationalised by the Czech government, which was itself newly liberated from German control. It remained in government (Communist) hands for the next 46 years and its production lines of tractors, motorcycles, trucks and cars expanded or contracted according to government decrees rather than in response to demand.

While capitalism in western Europe became increasingly adept at encouraging people to buy cleaning products they didn't need, in order to polish gadgets that they hadn't known they wanted, much of eastern Europe was languishing under Soviet control, oblivious to the insidious charms of consumerism.

In the Czech Republic there were very few cars to buy, no advertisements and limited television. There was no need for selling techniques designed to distract attention from a daft-sounding name, or to employ branding 'creatives' to come up with a better one. It was a sellers' market – after paying the equivalent of several months' salary and then waiting a decade for the banger, buyers were expected to be grateful. They certainly were.

It was during this period that the Skoda joke achieved its currency. For example, and with apologies: 'What do you do if you and your Skoda are attacked by a swarm of killer bees?' Answer: 'Stop pushing and climb into the car for shelter.' Or: 'Why do Skodas have back windscreen wipers?' 'To clear off the flies that rear-end them.' Or: 'How do you double the value of your Skoda?' 'Fill the tank with petrol.'

But since 1991, when the Czech Republic became a market economy, the quality of the cars has improved, making them enormously popular – so the last and longest laugh is Skoda's, and it's on us. It has survived the vicissitudes of European history and remains a manufacturing business with a dodgy name that sells a great many cars. When one of its witty advertising campaigns next makes you chortle at the Skoda name in a self-referential, self-mocking way, consider that the cost of the ads is paid ultimately by the people who buy the cars.

Equally, without the Skoda jokes that kept the brand name alive during the eighties, awareness of the name wouldn't be what it is today. Ask yourself how many other brands from former Eastern bloc countries you can think of, and why Volkswagen chose to keep 'Skoda' when they could just as easily have discarded it.

'Intellectual property is arguably what has become most important to business over the last hundred years', says Peter Matthews of Nucleus, the London branding firm we encountered in the previous chapter.

'Manufacturing in Western economies has been on a sharp slide since the Second World War and although the service sector has become increasingly important, service jobs are just as easy to outsource from Europe as manufacturing jobs these days. Hence the growth of call centres in places like India. So what does the West still have? It has intellectual property – its ideas and the quality of its craftsmanship.'

'Take a pair of Jimmy Choo shoes and a pair of shoes from George at Asda, the supermarket. One might retail at £400.00 and the other at £14.99. The cost of the raw materials might be slightly higher for the Jimmy Choos, but that doesn't account for the vast difference in price. The rest of it is the quality of the craftsmanship, which is intellectual property in the sense that someone has to learn how to make the shoes by hand, and the name of the brand itself.'

'The equity in the brand is the intellectual property. Jimmy Choo could manufacture their shoes in Shanghai rather than Italy and still charge the same for a pair of shoes that was substantially cheaper to make. The difference in profit would remain in Western hands either way because of the intellectual property involved.'

'What's in a name?' fourteen-year-old Juliet enquired of the sweet night air. In Shakespeare's day, a rose by any other name could smell as sweet ... but not to us, not any more. Skoda cars still travel the highways and autobahns of Europe precisely because our obsession with what used to be meaningless detail – name recognition – has become an intrinsic part of our way of life. Without it and the laws that uphold intellectual property rights, the difference between standards of living in Europe and elsewhere would be eroding far more quickly than it is. In this sense, our obsession with branding has come to underpin our affluence.

And now, in the spirit of a television programme that shows out-takes during the closing credits, here is a small selection of products whose names qualified them for entry into the 'Black Museum' of one west London advertising agency.

English-speaking consumers nearly received, on their supermarket shelves in recent years, a brand of marshmallow manufactured for the Danish market called 'Skum Banana', a delicious Spanish potato chip named – rather musically – 'Bum', a Danish chewing gum called 'Sor-bits' and a Latin American poultry dish called 'Cock Soup'. And last, but by no means least, somewhere in the vastness of Latin America there's a canned tuna, endorsed on the label with the words 'Grated Fanny'. These products are all genuine and put the plangent 'Skoda' into the shade.

# Hitler planned to move Nelson's Column to a spot in Berlin

Operation Sealion was the name given to the planned Nazi invasion of Britain, which Hitler originally planned for 1940. France had fallen, the Channel Islands were occupied and to achieve a total victory in Europe without being harried from the west, Hitler knew it would have to be done.

On 16 July 1940, he issued Führer Directive No. 16, 'Preparations for a landing operation against Britain', with a target date of 15 September that year. It didn't take place, largely because of preparations for a massive assault on the Eastern front. But the fact that this document exists makes a favourite scenario of literature and film – what if Britain had been invaded by the Nazis? – a little less vicarious. It existed on paper and, therefore, concretely in the minds of those who would have perpetrated it.

The British are a little freaky about the Second World War: has there actually been an edition of *The Times* over the last 60 years in which the word 'Nazi' hasn't appeared? But it was one of the biggest events of the 20th century and if Germany had won the war, the world would be a very different place today, so can you really blame us? Thoughts of this alternative reality are perhaps commonplace, but when the details emerge from virtual history's flickering shadows, they become less so.

A second document, entitled 'Plans for England', was prepared by Department III of the German Security Service and dated 26 August 1940. 'Ever since the battle of Trafalgar', it said, 'the Nelson Column has represented for England a symbol of British naval might and world domination. It would be an impressive way of underlining the German victory if the Column were to be moved to Berlin.'

This was about brutal symbolism – the 'great man' theory of history writ large. Had it come to pass, it would have been one historical colossus, Hitler, appropriating the effigy of another in order to make a further symbolic point. Nelson prevented a possible Napoleonic invasion of Britain by winning at Trafalgar and effectively wiping out the French and Spanish navies. He made the seas safe for British commerce and created the conditions that allowed British imperialism to flourish. By the late 19th century, one could accurately say that the sun never set on the British Empire. Maps of the globe were disproportionately pink, and Karl Marx, scribbling away in north London, was tolerated in ways that he hadn't been on the continent because, by any rational measure, he was no threat to his self-confident host nation. (There's a lesson in there somewhere.)

Nelson's victory at Trafalgar is seen as crucial to Britain's unprecedented imperial prosperity, so uprooting Nelson's statue and its 170-foot column to take it to Berlin would have been an appalling blow to British morale after a successful invasion: a jack-boot grinding an already pulped face. Hitler's capture of this ultimate symbol of empire would have been pointing out that he had succeeded where Napoleon failed.

The occupation ordinances make fascinating reading, as described in *If Britain Had Fallen* by Norman Longmate, a book that accompanied a 1970s television series. Bureaucrats in Berlin made incredibly detailed plans about occupying Britain; for instance, how to administer fishing rights on British inland waterways. The same document suggested that all British able-bodied men between the ages of seventeen and 45 should be dispatched to the Continent as slave labour, ensuring that the rest of the population would remain subdued. And very few of Britain's 450,000 Jews would have seen the end of the decade.

Bizarrely, though, the city of Birmingham was singled out for praise by this how-to manual for the everyday invasion. 'Good propaganda material in German is published there', it said, mystifyingly, adding that the information bureau run by the city council was 'a very valuable institute of which little public notice is taken'. In the same vein, the author, who was clearly in the business of laying the foundations of an efficient bureaucracy, recommended that in the event of a successful invasion, a certain 'Fraulein F', formerly of a Hamburg firm, would become invaluable. Her ability to perform shorthand and typing in English would, apparently, have been of nearly limitless use to the German authorities in Britain.

'When arresting Englishmen', the ordinances continued, 'it is important to apprehend their servants. Every distinguished

Englishman has a valet, often an ex-regular soldier, who is usually exceptionally well-informed on the private and official affairs of his master.' Despite the idiocy of this in the middle of a war that had already seen conscription introduced, the documentation hints at the kind of intimate knowledge that the Nazis would have used to detect and condemn anti-occupation activists, as indeed they did elsewhere. The walls wouldn't have needed ears.

If the Germans had adopted the same policy that they did in France (occupying the industrialised, highly populated part of the country and the national capital and choosing a spa town as the capital of the puppet regime), Britain's Vichy, it was suggested by historian Andrew Roberts in an essay on Hitler's Britain, could well have been Harrogate. The enormous Victorian hotels, such as the Cairn, Crown, Majestic, Old Swan, Granby and Imperial, might have housed government ministries. And from there, campaigns could have been orchestrated to destroy important British cultural organisations, including trade unions, Masonic lodges, public schools, the Church of England and the Scout movement.

The texture of everyday life under an imaginary Nazi occupation of Britain has also been thoroughly well imagined in fiction. Len Deighton's thriller *SS-GB* is especially strong on this – the author piles detail upon detail to create a convincing alternative reality. In this version the King is imprisoned in the Tower of London and Churchill has been executed by firing squad, rumoured to have refused a blindfold and raised his two fingers in a V for victory as the order to shoot was given.

Our hero, a Scotland Yard detective known in deliciously period fashion as 'Archer of the Yard', is morally compromised by his perceived collaboration with the German forces of law. He watches Nazi soldiers surround a little school – one of the teachers is a known resistance activist and all the teachers and some older pupils are to be interned as a result. The psychology of being detained en masse by the Gestapo along with one's colleagues is chillingly rendered in a London suburb.

And Robert Harris's *Fatherland* deals with a Europe in which the reality of the 'final solution' remains unknown because the Nazis won the war: there's merely a rumour of mass exodus, biblical style, to the east. It's the 1960s and British maids are fashionable in

Berlin, as are French chefs, Ukrainian street sweepers and Polish gardeners (so what's different, you may well ask?). King Edward VIII sits on the throne of England alongside his consort, formerly known as Mrs Simpson, and President Kennedy – Joseph, not Jack – looks good for a man of 75. Plausibly, considering Nazi punctiliousness in administrative matters, this thriller follows a government paper trail leading another compromised policeman hero to discover the big lie at the heart of his society. At one stage the trail takes him past the European Parliament in Berlin. 'The flags of the twelve member nations were lit by spots. The swastika which flew above them was twice the size of the other standards', wrote Harris in 1991, poking fun at the EU in a manner that's now slightly dated by the number of members.

Films including *Went the Day Well?* (1942) and *It Happened Here* (1966) cover the same subject, as do the novels *Loss of Eden* by Douglas Brown and Christopher Serpell (1940*)*, *I, James Blunt* by H.V. Morton (1940) and *If Hitler had Invaded England* by C.S. Forester (1971).

The Nazi list of political enemies to be dealt with upon their arrival in London included Noël Coward, whose later play *Peace in Our Time* (1947) focuses on the war. The writer Rebecca West was also on the list – when she found out, she famously telegraphed Coward, saying: 'My dear, the people we should have been seen dead with!' Her good humour is a reminder of what would have been lost in the event that the Nazis' *Sonderfahndungsliste GB*, or 'special search list' had been put to any practical use. In addition to obvious political figures based in London at the time – Churchill, Eden and de Gaulle – the list also named H.G. Wells, Virginia Woolf, Aldous Huxley (who had been living in America since 1936), J.B. Priestley, C.P. Snow, Stephen Spender and the publisher Victor Gollancz.

But what of a different virtual history question: what would the world be like if Nelson had lost the Battle of Trafalgar and never achieved the pinnacle of fame that elevated him 170 feet in the air in central London? There would be no Nelson's Column and certainly no Trafalgar Square – not in Britain, at least. In fact, it's possible that after a century and a half of Britain being administered by the French, Operation Sealion wouldn't have been necessary at all, because by 1940 the British capital would already have been Vichy.

# 50 Facts that Should Change the World

## Jessica Williams

- A third of the world is at war

- Cars kill two people every minute

- America spends more on pornography than it does on foreign aid

- More than 150 countries use torture

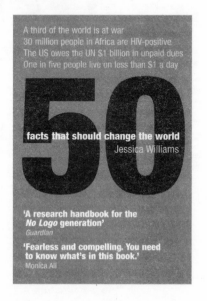

Think you know what's going on in the world?

Jessica Williams will make you think again.

Read about hunger, poverty, human rights abuses, unimaginable wealth, the drugs trade, corruption, gun culture, the abuse of our environment and much more in this shocking bestseller.

'A research handbook for the *No Logo* generation'  *Guardian*
'Fearless and compelling. You need to know what's in this book.'  Monica Ali

Paperback £9.99

ISBN: 1 84046 547 6

# 101 Facts You Should Know About Food

## John Farndon

Attention-grabbing facts and
punchy popular analysis of the
things you really should know
about the food you eat.

- The largest modern fishing
  trawler drags a net twice the
  volume of the Millennium Dome
- A jar of instant coffee costs
  7,000 per cent more than the
  farmer receives for it
- High-yielding turkeys have such
  large breasts they cannot have
  sex
- A single fast food meal causes
  similar changes in brain chemistry
  to class A drugs
- The biggest beneficiaries of the EU's farm subsidies are not
  farmers but food manufacturers

From the extraordinary distance most of our food travels to reach our
tables to the remarkable benefits of eating tomatoes, John Farndon
shows the amazing, often shocking, truth behind the food we eat.
Covering everything from the big businesses that control food production
around the world to the dangers of food dyes, this book reveals the
complex facts behind the simplest of meals.

Find out just what GM food is and why you may eat it unknowingly, how
food gets its flavour, how some foods are not quite as nutritious as they
should be, how bringing exotic foods to your table may literally be
costing the Earth, and much more.

This is an essential guide to the facts behind food, the one vital thing in
your life besides air and water – and the world's biggest business.

Paperback £6.99

ISBN 10: 1 84046 767 3     ISBN 13: 978 1840467 67 3

# Iran: Everything You Need to Know

## John Farndon

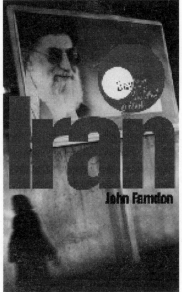

- Could Iran build and use nuclear weapons?
- Might London become the target of an Iranian nuclear attack?
- How would we be affected if Iran cut off oil supplies?
- Does the West's attitude drive young Iranians to extremism?

Iran's President shocked the West when he described the Holocaust as a myth and called for Israel to be 'wiped off the map'. No wonder then that some Western leaders are terrified at the prospect of Iran resuming its nuclear programme – and perhaps building nuclear weapons.

Many argue that Iran is a huge danger. But are the doomsayers right? Is Iran the rabid Islamic dog that some paint it? Is it in fact, as others say, the most prosperous, sophisticated, cultured nation in the Middle East?

*Iran: Everything You Need to Know* gives you the facts and lets you form your own opinion on this crucial world issue.

Paperback £5.99

ISBN 10: 1 84046 776 2    ISBN 13: 978 1840467 76 5

# Bird Flu: Everything You Need to Know

## John Farndon

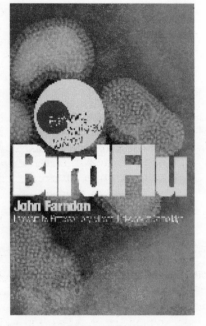

A bird flu pandemic is inevitable – so we are told. First identified in China, this apparently merciless virus which originated in chickens has the potential to mutate, possibly killing thousands, even millions, of people. But how accurate is this picture? Is it a panic created by the media or a genuine threat against which we should protect ourselves immediately – and how can we do this?

Whether you are worried about the implications of bird flu for you and your family, or you are simply interested in learning more than what you see and read in the media, this book is for you.

Paperback £5.99

ISBN: 1 84046 749 5

# China: Friend or Foe?

## Hugo de Burgh

China is growing
phenomenally, with half the
world's cranes currently on its
soil. Its 1.3 billion people have
around 300 million mobile
phones and a purchasing
power second only to the US,
although, especially in rural
areas, there is widespread
poverty. Government
censorship is a fact of life –
with 30,000 workers manning
a firewall restricting citizens'
access to the internet.

Yet few in the West know
much about China. Popular
press coverage is limited to stereotypes, the serious media to
economics and business, and that's about it. What *does* China
mean to the rest of the world?

Hugo de Burgh explores the key questions: How is China
managed? How does the Party function? What do we need to
know about Chinese nationalism? Will the Chinese economy
provide huge new opportunities for trade, or will it kill off our own
livelihoods? How is China using its political and cultural
influence? What about China's human rights record?

Is China a friend to be welcomed or a foe to be guarded against?
Accessible, straightforward and often astonishing, *China: Friend
or Foe?* is the first popular exploration of one of the biggest
issues of the next hundred years.

Paperback £7.99

ISBN 10: 1 84046 733 9     ISBN 13: 978 1840467 33 8

# Why Do People Hate America?

## Ziauddin Sardar and Merryl Wyn Davies

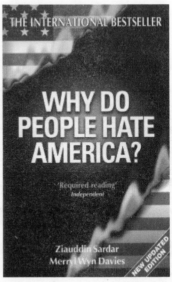

The economic power of US corporations and the virus-like power of American popular culture affect the lives and infect the indigenous cultures of millions around the world. The foreign policy of the US government, backed by its military strength, has unprecedented global influence now that the USA is the world's only superpower – its first 'hyperpower'.

America also exports its value systems, defining what it means to be civilised, rational, developed and democratic – indeed, what it is to be human. Meanwhile, the US itself is impervious to outside influence, and if most Americans think of the rest of the world at all, it is in terms of deeply ingrained cultural stereotypes.

Many people *do* hate America, in the Middle East and the developing countries as well as in Europe. Ziauddin Sardar and Merryl Wyn Davies explore the global impact of America's foreign policy and its corporate and cultural power, placing this unprecedented dominance in the context of America's own perception of itself. Their analysis provides an important contribution to a debate which needs to be addressed by people of all nations, cultures, religions and political persuasions.

Paperback £7.99

ISBN 1 84046 525 5

# Number Freaking

## Gary Rimmer

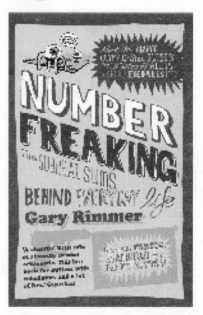

'A cheerful little mix of absurdly precise arithmetic. This is a book for nutters with calculators and a lot of fun.' *Guardian*

'Gary Rimmer is the Sam Spade of number puzzles, an ambassador for freaking figures, a one-man waterfall of bizarre maths facts.' *Sunday Telegraph*

From sex and celebrity to science and sport – Number Freaking provides the answers to every question you never needed to ask.

- When will America collide with Japan?
- Why did Elvis really die?
- What's a decent girlfriend worth?
- Which is more crowded: Jakarta, Ikea or Hell?
- How many people on Earth are drunk right now?

Discover for yourself how far you walk in a lifetime, how many people have ever lived and how to cure world debt in the ultimate guide to modern life ...

Paperback £7.99

ISBN 10: 1 84046 751 7    ISBN 13: 978 1840467 51 2

# The Lying Ape

## Brian King

'We have no plans to raise taxes'

'Botox will erase the effects of time'

'World War II bomber found on the moon'

'I love you'

Brian King, co-author of the bestselling *Beyond Coincidence*, unravels our all-embracing culture of lies and deception in this brilliant expose of the duplicity of modern life.

We are all natural born liars, telling an average of six lies a day. So the next time you speak to someone, the chances are that you will tell a lie. Or that you will be lied to.

In this witty and incisive new book, Brian King unravels the full extent of the deceit that surrounds us. he explores the deceptions of obvious candidates such as politicians, ad-men, journalists and second-hand car salesmen a well as the subtler falsehoods of our partners and children, including the white lies we all tell each other to preserve our previous self-esteem.

He also looks at some of the great liars of history, reveals how scientists can observe the brain as it suppresses the awkward truth in favour of the convenient lie, and advises on the best techniques for spotting a lie through body language and verbal slips.

The child who denies raiding the biscuit jar is actin on the same instinct as the prime minister who lies about weapons of mass destruction ...

Hardback £9.99

ISBN 10: 1 84046 736 3     ISBN 13: 978 1840467 36 9